MW01068335

Poems and Prose

GEORG TRAKL

Poems and Prose

A Bilingual Edition

Translated from the German
and with an introduction and notes by

Alexander Stillmark

 Northwestern University Press
Evanston, Illinois

Northwestern University Press
Evanston, Illinois 60208-4170

Published 2005 by Northwestern University Press. Translation, introduction,
and notes copyright © 2001 by Alexander Stillmark. First published 2001 by Libris.
All rights reserved.

Printed in the United States of America

10 9 8 7 6 5 4 3 2 1

ISBN 0-8101-2006-2

Library of Congress Cataloging-in-Publication data are available from the
Library of Congress.

The paper used in this publication meets the minimum requirements of the
American National Standard for Information Sciences – Permanence of Paper
for Printed Library Materials, ANSI Z39.48-1992.

CONTENTS

POEMS AND PROSE POEMS

Poems / Gedichte

Sebastian in a Dream / Sebastian im Traum

The Autumn of the Lonely / Der Herbst des Einsamen

Sevenfold Song of Death / Siebengesang des Todes

Song of the Recluse / Gesang des Abgeschiedenen

Poems from *Der Brenner*, 1914/15

Other poems published in Trakl's lifetime

Poems, 1912–1914, published posthumously

FOR
FRAUKE

'Knowledge is attained only by the one who despises happiness': this aphoristic saying, which would seem to lay claim to universal validity, is the characteristic expression of a poet whose vision of existence was marked both by courage and despair. A man of exceptional and vulnerable sensibility, Georg Trakl's inner life was torn by conflicts and extremes. Those who knew him personally all in some sense stood in awe of him. Rilke asked in wonderment 'who might he have been?' and imagined him as an outsider living in an almost mythical dimension, an 'excluded being' who 'experienced even what was close at hand as though pressed against panes of glass'. Trakl's fellow-poet Elsa Lasker-Schüler wrote tentatively of him in a dedicatory poem:

> His eyes looked very distant.
> As a young boy he had once been in heaven.

There was something about his nature as a poet that recalled Hölderlin or Novalis, both high priests of their vocation, and minds to which he felt drawn by subtle affinities. For in him too the inner vision, the image-making faculty, took precedence over the mimetic. Ludwig von Ficker, a literary friend who knew him more intimately than most, reported that 'he, though a strong drinker and drug taker, was never deserted by his noble, extraordinarily steely mental attitude'. Another close friend from his schooldays, Erhard Buschbeck, wrote with empathy in *Georg Trakl – Ein Requiem* of the poet who would often shun the world yet embrace the idea of death most willingly. He also accentuated Trakl's great integrity: 'Here is a man of truth who shatters every lie.' These disparate qualities of reclusiveness, aesthetic sensibility, intellectual resilience and resolute dedication to the veracity of the word, combined in him to produce a body of poetry which today stands out as one of the landmarks of twentieth-century European literature. When the philosopher Ludwig Wittgenstein, who generously acted as Trakl's benefactor during years of hardship, first read his poems he freely confessed: 'I don't understand them. But their *tone* delights me. It is the tone of true men of genius.'

Though a great deal has been made of the obscurity of Trakl's poems, and of the difficulty of their interpretation, it may be helpful initially to approach them by attuning oneself to their mood and tone. The intrinsic musicality of

Trakl's diction is strikingly evident from his earliest writings. This manifestly musical poet, who was captivated by Schoenberg's new doctrine of harmony, would generally compose in the minor key, for the vision of life projected by him is predominantly sombre and tragic. Like his Austrian forebear Nikolaus Lenau, the melancholy bard of autumn, Trakl insistently dwells on dissolution and decay. Yet it would be a hasty simplification to perceive no element of hope, no glint of redemptive light in that vision of encircling gloom. The poet's imaginative range is larger and more differentiated than may be deduced from the reading of a mere handful of poems. The resilient strength and formal purism evident in his handling of the poetic medium are themselves the surest attestation of a powerful artistic purpose and will. Even if death and corruption, transience and pain, are dominant themes in this poetry, the very lyricism itself constitutes a harmonizing and assuaging counter-force. The contrast in so much of Trakl between the harsh, metallic dissonances and the mellifluous and melodic qualities is an indication of the depth and variety of his art. The fruitful tensions between harmony and disharmony within his diction are among the richest sources of his poetic expressiveness. Trakl belongs among those modernist writers of the early twentieth century, following in the wake of Poe, Baudelaire and Rimbaud, whose aesthetics ran counter to the classical idea of beauty, who paid tribute to the Aesthetic of the Ugly and derived inspiration from what is decadent, corrupt and morbid. The notion of unalloyed beauty was wholly alien to Trakl's scheme of things, and he once asserted: 'one does well to resist perfect beauty.' In striving for absolute truth of expression, purity and precision of the word, he evolved a style, indeed almost a language of his own. It is the distinctiveness of that language, the specific gravity with which he endowed the word, the insistent patterns and images he produced, the intensity of expression he achieved, which give his poetry its status. This great concentration on expressiveness and dedicated service to the word endeared him to Karl Kraus, that passionate champion of the purity of language.

Georg Trakl was born in Salzburg on 3 February 1887, the fourth of six children, to Maria and Tobias Trakl, the latter successful in his business as an ironmonger, so that the young Trakl grew up in comfortable middle-class circumstances. The baroque city of Salzburg with its many musical associations, but also a place filled with vivid imagery of the twin forces of life and death, was to remain a haunting presence in the early poetry. The intimate relations which existed between the poet and the youngest of his siblings, Margarete, were to burden him with a sense of guilt which enters into his poems transmuted to a universalized motif of the tragic flaw in the human condition. Though baptized a Lutheran and instructed in that faith, he attended the school affiliated to the city's Catholic teachers' training college. After a somewhat unpromising career at the State Grammar School in Salzburg (where he failed to reach the required standard in Latin, Greek and Mathematics), he left without taking the 'Abitur' and embarked instead on a two-year course in Pharmacy at the University of Vienna. In 1906 he made his literary debut with the lyrical sketch 'Dreamland'. After initial disappointments with his early literary efforts there followed a period of withdrawal and experimentation with strong narcotics; a habit that could more readily be fed through his profession as a pharmacist. The period 1908–1911 embraces his four semesters at Vienna university ending in the quali-fication Magister Pharmaciae and his one year as a volunteer for military service. The year 1910 also marks the period at which Trakl finds his voice as a lyric poet: the development is rapid, and mastery of a unique, self-assured style (Trakl speaks of his 'arduously won manner') is brought to fruition as though guided by an inner logic. While all efforts to settle into a career and to find some material stability were constantly disappointed, the firm links Trakl established with the periodical *Der Brenner* in Innsbruck and the circle of literati associated with it (Ludwig von Ficker, Carl Dallago, Karl Barromäus Heinrich, Karl Röck) proved fruitful in terms of friendship and personal support. From now on an uninterrupted stream of his poems is first published in the pages of this bi-monthly journal. In 1912 a group of friends and admirers tried to organize a collected edition of his poetry with the publisher Albert Langen, to be entitled *Twilight and Decay*, but this venture came to nothing. In July 1913 the Leipzig publisher Kurt Wolff was to bring out Trakl's first volume of poems. This consisted of a selection made by Franz Werfel at the publisher's request and placed in the series *Der Jüngste Tag* ('Day of Judgement') under the simple title 'Poems'. A fuller collection, selected and ordered by the poet himself and entitled *Sebastian im Traum* ('Sebastian in a Dream'), was planned simultaneously but this was delayed by the outbreak of war and appeared only in July 1915, seven months after the author's death. The correspondence with Kurt Wolff shows Trakl's fastid-ious concern as to which poems should be excluded or replaced as well as to questions of their arrangement and presentation. He stipulated an Antiqua typeface, 'which gives a calm appearance to the type and one I believe appropriate to the nature of the poems' (April/May 1914). The ordering of the sequence of his poems was also a significant aspect of the poet's sense of total design and composition. Words, images, structures and motifs, are seen to carry over from poem to poem and thus to establish a cyclical flow. It is this striking inner coherence and over-arching formal structure in Trakl which moved Martin Heidegger to make the notorious generalization – at best a half-truth – that Trakl's work essentially consists of one poem. The last two years of Trakl's life were, taken as a whole, full of uncertainty, material insecurity, despondency and despair and he would keep returning to Innsbruck for friendship and consolation. They were, at the same time, the period of his fulfilment as a poet; the years when he produced 'Helian', *Sebastian im Traum*, the major prose poems 'Dream and Derangement' and 'Revelation and Perdition' and an abundance of fine poems for *Der Brenner*.

The year 1914, the last of Trakl's life, brought him little beyond painful experience and an encroaching sense of doom. His beloved sister Margarete, now married and living in Berlin, fell mortally ill and the impoverished poet felt utter despair at his helplessness. His attempts to raise money by borrowing proved futile and humiliating. Various schemes to emigrate, whether to Albania or to the Dutch East Indies, and find some employment were equally fruitless and dispiriting. Only his connections with *Der Brenner* served as an anchor and life-line to which he could hold. The assassination of Crown Prince Franz Ferdinand at Sarajevo on 28 June, which precipitated the calamity of the First World War, also ushered in the final chapter of Trakl's brief life. Joining up as an orderly in the Medical Corps, he was posted to the Eastern Front in Galicia during late August and had his first harrowing experience of the aftermath of battle at Grodek. Placed in sole charge of ninety gravely wounded soldiers in a makeshift field hospital, lacking all medical support and surrounded by the gruesome aspect of the dead and dying, he made an attempt to shoot himself which his comrades just managed to prevent. Some weeks later he was confined to a psychiatric clinic at Crakow for further observation. Fearful of being sentenced to death by Court Martial and increasingly suffering from depression, he took an overdose of cocaine and died on 3 November. He was buried three days later in the Rakoviecz Cemetery at Crakow. His remains were subsequently transferred to Mühlau near Innsbruck and laid to rest on 7 October 1925.

Trakl once described his poetic style as 'my pictorial manner which forges together four separate image-parts in four lines of a stanza into a single impression' (to Buschbeck, July 1910). This serial style is essentially cumulative in that it builds up its effects from discrete elements of language, and these are generally marked off from each other by a period which coincides with the end of a line. In the earlier poetry, up to 1912, the use of rhyme still predominates, and this helps to create further connections and associations within a poem. Thereafter Trakl abandons rhyme and creates his own freer rhythms, engendering lyricism by more varied and subtle means. The absence of rhyme in the maturer poetry intensifies the sense of separateness in the constituent elements of the poem so that fragmentation and compositeness are set at odds and new tensions result. One of the chief unifying agents in this poetry is the powerfully evocative image or symbol which the poet employs, not only with a sure sense of tradition and cultural heritage, but also with innovative force. The tradition to which he is deeply beholden is, of course, Christian and European; in short, all that the word 'Abendland' (the 'West') connoted for him in terms of civilization and culture. Yet 'the West' was no longer united or sustained by its heritage, and Trakl felt the void, sensed alienation and loss, more acutely perhaps than any poet since Hölderlin.

The figure of the unaccommodated, homeless man is recurrent in Trakl. The wanderer, the stranger, but also 'the unborn' (one who is not wholly of this world) are constant presences. The poet's self is hardly ever overtly present in Trakl's severely impersonal style. He avoids using the first person singular. Instead, the poetic persona enters the poem and a range of symbolic figures – Elis, Sebastian, Helian, Kaspar Hauser – stand in for the poetic self. This consistent objectivization of vision and feeling actually serves to heighten the emotive force vested in a poem. No less effective is the rhetorical device of apostrophe or invocation which Trakl repeatedly employs. The immediate impact of direct address, assisted by a conveyed sense of urgent emotion, feeds that incantatory quality which is a hallmark of this poet's style. As a reader, one is constantly aware of the presence of a speaking voice.

The figure of the young boy or youth, which abounds in these poems, serves as one form of distillation of the poet's consciousness. It is a figure distinguished by solitude and remoteness, deeply acquainted with grief and endowed with an aura of sacredness and purity. Suffering innocence is one of Trakl's major themes: its keynote is the perfect victim at Calvary but it is also given voice through the recurrent image of the bleeding prey, the hunter's quarry, the game that dies at the hand of man. The dark counterparts to this passive immolation are to be found in the powerfully active presence of guilt, evil, and death. The whole scheme of salvation-history embracing man's fall from grace, his corrupt state, his proneness to sin and guilt, has been assimilated into Trakl's store of imagery. His is a poetry of pity which rebels against the sacrilege of suffering in all creation. His sombre imagery, with its perpetual emphasis on the blackness of corruption and decay, connotes deep moral outrage at the staying power of evil in an unredeemed world. It was largely his reading of Dostoyevsky which inspired and nurtured in him that profound moral indignation bound to compassion. Trakl had read him avidly in the influential translation by E. K. Rahsin (published between 1906–1919 by R. Piper & Co., Munich) and saw in him the most powerful revolutionary intellectual force of his times. It is noteworthy that he also imbibed Nietzsche, who might be seen as Dostoyevsky's antipode, with comparable enthusiasm. He equally fell under the spell of Hölderlin's late vatic hymns with their cryptic language and stately free rhythms. Hölderlin's influence may partly be traced in a deeply-felt nostalgic relationship to biblical symbols and associations, the lure of myth and sacred legend, but above all in that grasp of the pure luminous image which we find in 'Patmos' and 'Der Einzige' ('The Only One'). Trakl's 'Helian' and the later poems derive something of their elevated diction and clarity of image from these models.

The dominant trend in much early criticism was to consider Trakl's use of imagery as 'hermetic', that is to say, sealed off from any system of meaning outside the referential framework of the poems themselves. Such a view accentuated the notion of the autonomy of the poet's language as though it were an abstract and artificial medium quite unrelated to common experience, to the traditions of poetry in general, or to established forms of symbolism in particular. It asserted the existence of a sort of poetic code within which any single poem might only be deciphered if examined in relation to the rest of the poet's work. While it is undoubtedly true that the interpretation of a Trakl poem is often illumined by adducing crucial and recurring formulations in other parts of the work, the idea that his perception of reality lacks sensuous dimensions or is divorced from the experiential is clearly untenable. The deepest sources of this poet's creative imagination appear always to spring from the sensuous self and to be intrinsically bound to a palpable world. True, he was not primarily concerned with the descriptive but with the archetypal in his imagery; with essences that lay beyond the visible world. That is why his language, with its uncertain syntactical relations, its unwonted grammar and elliptical contractions, is for ever reaching out for expressive means which transcend the phenomenal. In one revealing confessional letter to a friend (Hermine von Ranterberg, 5 October 1908) the young poet allows insight into the deeper stirrings of his sentient and imaginative self:

I felt, smelt, touched the most terrible possibilities within me, and heard the demons howl in my blood, the thousand devils with their spikes which madden the flesh. What a fearful nightmare!

Gone! Today this vision of reality has dissolved into nothing again, these things are far away from me, their voices farther still, and I listen enraptured once more to the melodies that live in me, and my elated eye again dreams up its images which are lovelier than all reality! My entire, beautiful world filled with infinite harmony.

The disturbing inner visions are vitally connected with the life of the senses and are mediated by a language imbued with the sensual. Yet when the poet is most at one with himself, his language aspires to the condition of music. How much he was absorbed and guided by purely sensuous sound in the language of poetry is attested by a review he wrote on a lesser known contemporary author, Gustav Streicher:

It is strange how these lines of verse penetrate the problem, how the sound of a word often expresses an unutterable thought and holds fast to the fleeting mood. There lies in these lines something of the sweet feminine power of persuasion which beguiles us to listen to the melos of the word and not to heed the content and weight of the word; the musical minor key of this language instils a pensiveness into the senses and fills the blood with dreamy tiredness.

In writing about another's style, Trakl is in fact divulging more about his own: the sensuous mellifluence to which he responds here is but an echo of his inner ideal.

Trakl was seldom, if ever, satisfied with the result of his writing. His perfectionism was such as to impel him to continual revision of his drafts so that the published version of a poem became the end-product of an arduous process of trial and error. To include all the variants in a collected edition would be trespassing upon the territory of textual scholarship proper. One representative example of this progressive genesis had to be included, however. The three versions of 'To Novalis' demonstrate how the poet's method of reworking both alters and reduces the material, condensing it to discrete images whose isolation is increased as conjunctions and adverbs are withdrawn. The nuclear words and images ('sacred youth', 'crystalline/dark earth', 'his flowering', 'sank low/fell silent') are retained yet new symbolic associations are tried out and then superseded. The strewing of palms – as a biblical reference – or the introduction of the blue flower – as the all-too familiar emblem of Romanticism – evidently seemed to the poet less expressive than the idea of the 'divine spirit' which he likens to the bud unfolding into a flower (and this too has its antecedent in Hölderlin). In the end, setting the three versions side by side, it is hard to say which is the superior poem.

Trakl's poetic style is characterized by repeated patterns, recurrent formulations, persistent images stamped by a clear and vivid imagination. Colours in particular are conspicuous throughout his poems and they are employed not naturalistically but rather with emotive and connotative force, their significance changing according to context. Even to attempt a valid generalization as to the spiritual or ethereal attributes contained in the much used term 'silvery', or the gloomy, corrupt, deathlike in 'black', or the vibrant intensity of the passions in 'scarlet', would be to fall prey to some reductive bias or simplification. The richly textured late prose poem 'Revelation and Perdition' – an excellent place to start for an exploration of Trakl's poetic practice – can provide numerous instances where colour is used as a mysterious attribute of no fixed meaning. But evocativeness, not fixity of meaning, is the province of genuine poetry. Trakl's individual and wilful use of colour symbolism shows us how language may be empowered and charged with new significance quite beyond conventional usage or expectation. Though not a fellow-traveller of Expressionism, to which he has occasionally been assigned by critics, partly through being included in Kurt Pinthus's famed anthology *Menschheitsdämmerung* (1920), a striking kinship with dominant trends in contemporary painting, particularly as regards the unconventional use of colour, may indeed be ascertained. The self-portrait Trakl painted in March 1914 during a time of acute spiritual crisis might well have been executed by Emil Nolde, so much does it reflect stylistic trends of the time. The grotesque, frozen features are simplified and accentuated to achieve a mask-like effect set against a background of luminous ghostly aquamarine. The deep blue shading on the face in coarse brushwork forms a stark contrast to the garish reds and browns of the highlighted parts. The overlarge eyes are mere empty hollows darkened with a dull and deathly blue. Only the lips seem to waver in sensitive uncertainty. As an image of the self this mask expresses deepest withdrawal and gloomy isolation. The technique is wholly in line with that bold experimentation with colour symbolism to be found among leading contemporary painters such as Franz Marc, August Macke, Kandinsky and Chagall.

Standing as he does at the threshold of a century destined to outrival all that went before in the horrors of revolution, war and the wholesale wastage of humankind, Trakl may be seen as the sombre visionary of the modern age.

The melancholy and elegiac moods that predominate in his poetry herald the calamity of the First World War and its dire consequences. The five powerful poems he wrote on the subject of war ('Mankind', 'Trumpets', 'In the East', 'Lament', 'Grodek') are prophetic in tone and filled with imagery of ruin and dereliction. 'Mankind', written in 1912 before Trakl had experienced actual warfare, is resonant with apocalyptic foreboding. Stark images of destruction and violence are meaningfully juxtaposed with devotional imagery which highlights the notions of human guilt and its atonement through the wounds of a sacrificial act. At its conclusion, St Thomas, the figure of doubt and lack of faith, stands ultimately for all humanity. The recurrent scarlet banners in 'Trumpets' are the blood-soaked symbols of the fanatical madness of war. The ferocity of the forces of destruction evoked by 'In the East' culminates in an image which expresses the triumph of the beast: 'Wild wolves burst through the gate'. 'Lament' and 'Grodek' – the last poems Trakl wrote – dwell with moving intensity on death, not as an instant of release but as a lingering nightmare filled with visions in which grandeur and bloodshed, beauty and torment combine. The mythical personification of Night in both poems, which suggests a calm and eternal presence, has an element of consolation in it. Yet the dominant note in each is one of grief at the destruction of life and wholeness. Trakl imbues the theme of mourning with a degree of dignity and stateliness quite distinct from the triumphalist and celebratory hymns with which other poets of the day (including Rilke in his 'Five Songs') greeted the outbreak of war. Trakl's last poems are not war poems in the conventional sense at all, but rather sonorous threnodies which mourn the violation of the image of man. By virtue of their apocalyptic accents and images they are wholly consistent with the main body of the poet's work. If one turns to Trakl's letters for some insight into his oppressed state of mind during the latter part of his life, one is startled by the virulence of his self-loathing and the bleakness of his despair:

Too little love, too little justice and mercy, and always too little love; all too much hardness, arrogance, and all manner of criminality – that's me. I'm certain I only avoid evil out of weakness and cowardice and so further shame my wickedness. I long for the day when the soul shall cease to wish or be able to live in this wretched body polluted with melancholy, when it shall quit this laughable form made of muck and rottenness, which is all too faithful a reflection of a godless, cursed century (to Ludwig von Ficker, 26 June 1913).

If it is true, as has often been claimed, that the poet is the seismograph of his times, then the correspondence between self and world which may be gleaned from this confession is of the closest. Though supremely sensitive to the symptoms of the age, though aggrieved and alienated by so much that the world held in store, Trakl bravely confronts even the direst moments of experience through his poetry. The utter dedication to his art and the almost religious significance he attached to it may be seen reflected in the following succinct formulation of his convictions:

Feeling at moments of deathlike being; all human beings are worthy of love. Waking you feel the bitterness of the world; therein lies all your unresolved guilt; your poem an imperfect penance.

There is perhaps no surer approach to close scrutiny of a poem than to attempt a translation. The process itself, with all its requisite reflections, choices, checks and revisions, amounts, in essence, to an act of interpretation. Whether one chooses to aim at a plain prosaic translation or what Goethe called 'the parodistic' (which attempts to capture the strangeness of the foreign meaning), or one aspires to make the translation identical with the original so that it can fully replace it, the effort will always remain an approximation. Dryden, using a pictorial simile, maintained that 'translation is a kind of Drawing after Life' which, whilst aiming at a true likeness, at its best will only imply a 'bringing nearer' to the original. Indeed, it might generally be asserted that, given the richness and complexity of the language of poetry, the words of a translator only partly 'cover' the meanings created by the poet. The present is an attempt to achieve as truthful a rendering of Trakl's language as possible: one which is linguistically accurate, which is attentive to the particular 'weight' this poet gives to the word, which reflects the strangeness of his diction and syntax and renders the general 'feel' of his distinctive style. Since the reproduction of rhyme, even in the minority of poems where it exists, would work against these principles, it has not been attempted. The visionary, often dream-like language with which a world is pieced together by the poet challenges the translator at every turn. The particular resonance and intensity of Trakl's diction is such that it may be emulated but scarcely reproduced. The many unresolved ambiguities and indefinite syntactical relations – which are of course always intended – no less than his idiosyncratic punctuation and neologisms, all needed to find some near-equivalence in the English. The great benefit of a bilingual edition comes into its own especially where a reader wishes to address these inherent complexities. One of the outstanding features of Trakl's diction – the repetition of vocabulary – also needed to be dealt with consistently. If an occasional deviation from a repeated word, some shift of accentuation, seemed justified, it was prompted by the context or maybe by a need to lend more stress (as with the colours 'red', 'scarlet', 'blood-red', for instance, or 'dark', 'darkness', 'gloom'). The poet's predilection for elevated poetic terms like 'Antlitz', 'Odem' or 'Woge', needed to be respected where possible, but it is scarcely feasible to reproduce in English every original compound coinage, the dynamics of certain prefixes ('hinfliesst', 'anfällt', 'umdüstert') or a number of indefinite abstract substantives ('ein Schweigendes', 'ein Abgelebtes', 'Einsames', 'Glühendes'). Trakl's penchant for alliterative effects, his rather languid cadences, and the melancholy music of his vowel sounds may, of course, be attempted if never properly re-created in another language. Above all, the fuller connotations of a word employed by so subtle and innovative a poet are almost inevitably going to undergo a sea-change when transferred to another culture.

Despite these inevitable difficulties, the wish to acquaint an English readership with a major poet whose work has not yet reached the wider audience it deserves, is the overriding concern of this edition. It comprises the greater body of poetry Trakl completed in his lifetime without the juvenilia or variants: i.e. the bulk of *Gedichte* (1913), the complete collection *Sebastian im Traum* (1915), all poems published in *Der Brenner* (1914–15), twenty-one further poems written between 1912–1914, and the entire prose for the first time. A few of these have appeared in print elsewhere: twelve in *Viribus Unitis. Festschrift für Bernhard Stillfried*, Peter Lang (Bern, Vienna, 1996) and nine in *Modern Poetry in Translation*, New Series No. 8, King's College London, Autumn 1999, and a further selection in No. 16, Spring 2000.

Poems and Prose

DIE RABEN

Über den schwarzen Winkel hasten
Am Mittag die Raben mit hartem Schrei.
Ihr Schatten streift an der Hirschkuh vorbei
Und manchmal sieht man sie mürrisch rasten.

O wie sie die braune Stille stören,
In der ein Acker sich verzückt,
Wie ein Weib, das schwere Ahnung berückt,
Und manchmal kann man sie keifen hören

Um ein Aas, das sie irgendwo wittern,
Und plötzlich richten nach Nord sie den Flug
Und schwinden wie ein Leichenzug
In Lüften, die von Wollust zittern.

IM ROTEN LAUBWERK VOLL GUITARREN...

Im roten Laubwerk voll Guitarren
Der Mädchen gelbe Haare wehen
Am Zaun, wo Sonnenblumen stehen.
Durch Wolken fährt ein goldner Karren.

In brauner Schatten Ruh verstummen
Die Alten, die sich blöd umschlingen.
Die Waisen süß zur Vesper singen.
In gelben Dünsten Fliegen summen.

Am Bache waschen noch die Frauen.
Die aufgehängten Linnen wallen.
Die Kleine, die mir lang gefallen,
Kommt wieder durch das Abendgrauen.

THE RAVENS

Across the black nook the ravens hasten
At noonday with harsh cry.
Their shadow sweeps past the hind
And sometimes one sees them in sullen repose.

O how they disturb the brown silence
Wherein a tilled field is enrapt
Like a woman by heavy foreboding entranced,
And sometimes one can hear them bickering

Over some carrion scented out somewhere;
Of a sudden they direct their flight northwards
And dwindle away like a funeral procession
In airs which shudder with rapture.

AMID RED FOLIAGE FULL OF GUITARS...

Amid red foliage full of guitars
The girls' yellow hair streams
Beside the fence where sunflowers stand.
Through clouds a golden cart passes.

In the repose of brown shadows, old folk
Grow silent in foolish embraces.
Orphans sweetly sing at vespers.
Flies buzz in the yellow vapours.

Along the brook women are washing still.
The hung-out linen gently flutters.
The young girl whom I long have fancied
Returns again through dusk at evening.

Vom lauen Himmel Spatzen stürzen
In grüne Löcher voll Verwesung.
Dem Hungrigen täuscht vor Genesung
Ein Duft von Brot und herben Würzen.

MUSIK IM MIRABELL

Zweite Fassung

Ein Brunnen singt. Die Wolken stehn
Im klaren Blau, die weißen, zarten.
Bedächtig stille Menschen gehn
Am Abend durch den alten Garten.

Der Ahnen Marmor ist ergraut.
Ein Vogelzug streift in die Weiten.
Ein Faun mit toten Augen schaut
Nach Schatten, die ins Dunkel gleiten.

Das Laub fällt rot vom alten Baum
Und kreist herein durchs offne Fenster.
Ein Feuerschein glüht auf im Raum
Und malet trübe Angstgespenster.

Ein weißer Fremdling tritt ins Haus.
Ein Hund stürzt durch verfallene Gänge.
Die Magd löscht eine Lampe aus,
Das Ohr hört nachts Sonatenklänge.

WINTERDÄMMERUNG

An Max von Esterle

Schwarze Himmel von Metall.
Kreuz in roten Stürmen wehen
Abends hungertolle Krähen
Über Parken gram und fahl.

Im Gewölk erfriert ein Strahl;
Und vor Satans Flüchen drehen
Jene sich im Kreis und gehen
Nieder siebenfach an Zahl.

Out of the mellow sky plunge sparrows
Into green holes full of corruption.
The hungry man's full restoration is gulled by
A waft of bread and pungent herbs.

MUSIC IN THE MIRABELL

Second version

A fountain sings. Clouds, white and tender,
Are set in the clear blueness
Engrossed, silent people walk
At evening through the ancient garden.

Ancestral marble has grown grey.
A flight of birds seeks far horizons.
A faun with lifeless pupils peers
At shadows gliding into darkness.

The leaves fall red from the old tree
And circle in through open windows.
A fiery gleam ignites indoors
And conjures up wan ghosts of fear.

A white stranger steps into the house.
A dog runs wild through ruined passages.
The maid extinguishes a lamp,
At night are heard sonata sounds.

DUSK IN WINTER

To Max von Esterle

Black metallic skies.
Crossing in red storms at eve
Hunger-maddened crows are blown
Over parkland grim and bare.

In the clouds a gleam is frozen;
And to Satan's curses they
Wheel full circle and go down
Sevenfold in number.

In Verfaultem süß und schal
Lautlos ihre Schnäbel mähen.
Häuser dräu'n aus stummen Nähen;
Helle im Theatersaal.

Kirchen, Brücken und Spital
Grauenvoll im Zwielicht stehen.
Blutbefleckte Linnen blähen
Segel sich auf dem Kanal.

RONDEL

Verflossen ist das Gold der Tage,
Des Abends braun und blaue Farben:
Des Hirten sanfte Flöten starben
Des Abends blau und braune Farben
Verflossen ist das Gold der Tage.

DIE SCHÖNE STADT

Alte Plätze sonnig schweigen.
Tief in Blau und Gold versponnen
Traumhaft hasten sanfte Nonnen
Unter schwüler Buchen Schweigen.

Aus den braun erhellten Kirchen
Schaun des Todes reine Bilder,
Großer Fürsten schöne Schilder.
Kronen schimmern in den Kirchen.

Rösser tauchen aus dem Brunnen.
Blütenkrallen drohn aus Bäumen.
Knaben spielen wirr von Träumen
Abends leise dort am Brunnen.

Mädchen stehen an den Toren,
Schauen scheu ins farbige Leben.
Ihre feuchten Lippen beben
Und sie warten an den Toren.

In corruption sweet and stale
Silently their beaks are scything.
Houses threaten mute and near;
Brightness in the amphitheatre.

Churches, bridge and hospital
Stand horrific in the twilight.
Blood-stained linen billows out
Sails upon the canal.

RONDELET

Departed is the gold of days,
The brown and the blue hues of evening;
The shepherd's gentle flutes have died
The blue and the brown hues of evening
Departed is the gold of days.

THE BEAUTIFUL CITY

Ancient squares in sunlit silence.
Deep engrossed in blue and gold
Dreamlike gentle nuns are hastening
Under sultry beeches' silence.

Out of brown illumined churches
Gaze pure images of death,
Lovely scutcheons of great princes.
Crowns are shimmering in the churches.

Horses rise out of the fountain.
Claws of blossom in trees threaten.
Boys confused in dreams are playing
Still at evening by the fountain.

Young girls standing in the gateways,
Shyly look upon life's gayness.
Their moist lips are ever trembling
And they wait beside the gateways.

Zitternd flattern Glockenklänge,
Marschtakt hallt und Wacherufen.
Fremde lauschen auf den Stufen.
Hoch im Blau sind Orgelklänge.

Helle Instrumente singen.
Durch der Gärten Blätterrahmen
Schwirrt das Lachen schöner Damen.
Leise junge Mütter singen.

Heimlich haucht an blumigen Fenstern
Duft von Weihrauch, Teer und Flieder.
Silbern flimmern müde Lider
Durch die Blumen an den Fenstern.

IM WINTER I

Der Acker leuchtet weiß und kalt.
Der Himmel ist einsam und ungeheuer.
Dohlen kreisen über dem Weiher
Und Jäger steigen nieder vom Wald.

Ein Schweigen in schwarzen Wipfeln wohnt.
Ein Feuerschein huscht aus den Hütten.
Bisweilen schellt sehr fern ein Schlitten
Und langsam steigt der graue Mond.

Ein Wild verblutet sanft am Rain
Und Raben plätschern in blutigen Gossen.
Das Rohr bebt gelb und aufgeschossen.
Frost, Rauch, ein Schritt im leeren Hain.

Fluttering sounds of bells are pealing,
Marching time and cries of watches.
Strangers listen on the stairways.
High in blueness organs pealing.

Bright-toned instruments are singing.
Through the leafy frame of gardens
Purls the laughter of fine women.
Quietly young mothers singing.

Secret breath by flowering windows
Smell of incense, tar and lilac.
Silvery tired eyelids flimmer
Through the flowers by the windows.

IN WINTER I

The ploughed earth sparkles white and cold.
The sky is lonely and immense.
Jackdaws circle above the pond
And huntsmen step down from the forest.

Among black tree-tops silence dwells.
A fiery glow flits from the huts.
At times sleigh bells ring from afar
And the grey moon is slow to rise.

Game gently bleeds to death by ridge
And ravens plash in gory gutters.
Reeds tremble yellow and erect.
Frost, smoke, a pace through empty grove.

ZU ABEND MEIN HERZ

Am Abend hört man den Schrei der Fledermäuse.
Zwei Rappen springen auf der Wiese.
Der rote Ahorn rauscht.
Dem Wanderer erscheint die kleine Schenke am Weg.
Herrlich schmecken junger Wein und Nüsse.
Herrlich: betrunken zu taumeln in dämmernden Wald.
Durch schwarzes Geäst tönen schmerzliche Glocken.
Auf das Gesicht tropft Tau.

MELANCHOLIE

Dritte Fassung

Bläuliche Schatten. O ihr dunklen Augen,
Die lang mich anschaun im Vorübergleiten.
Guitarrenklänge sanft den Herbst begleiten
Im Garten, aufgelöst in braunen Laugen.
Des Todes ernste Düsternis bereiten
Nymphische Hände, an roten Brüsten saugen
Verfallne Lippen und in schwarzen Laugen
Des Sonnenjünglings feuchte Locken gleiten.

VERKLÄRTER HERBST

Gewaltig endet so das Jahr
Mit goldnem Wein und Frucht der Gärten.
Rund schweigen Wälder wunderbar
Und sind des Einsamen Gefährten.

Da sagt der Landmann: Es ist gut.
Ihr Abendglocken lang und leise
Gebt noch zum Ende frohen Mut.
Ein Vogelzug grüßt auf der Reise.

Es ist der Liebe milde Zeit.
Im Kahn den blauen Fluß hinunter
Wie schön sich Bild an Bildchen reiht –
Das geht in Ruh und Schweigen unter.

AT EVENTIDE MY HEART

In the evening the cry of bats is heard.
Two black horses prance in the meadows.
The red sycamore rustles.
The wanderer chances on the little wayside inn.
Marvellous to the taste are young wine and nuts.
Marvellous. to reel drunken in the twilit forest.
Through black boughs painful bells peal.
Onto the face dewdrops fall.

MELANCHOLY

Third version

Bluish shadows. O you dark eyes
Which gaze long upon me gliding by.
Sounds of a guitar gently accompany autumn
In the garden, dissolved in brown fluids.
Death's grave darkling hour is prepared
By nymphen hands; decaying lips
Suck at red breasts and into black fluids
The sun-youth's damp locks glide.

TRANSFIGURED AUTUMN

The year has reached its mighty ending
With golden wine and fruit of gardens.
Forests around keep wondrous peace
And are companions to the lonely.

Then says the farmer: it is good.
You evening bells prolonged and quiet
Still at the last give us good heart.
A flock of birds hails on its journey.

It is the season mild of love.
Down the blue river in a boat
How image follows lovely image –
Then all goes down in rest and silence.

WINKEL AM WALD

An Karl Minnich

Braune Kastanien. Leise gleiten die alten Leute
In stilleren Abend; weich verwelken schöne Blätter.
Am Friedhof scherzt die Amsel mit dem toten Vetter,
Angelen gibt der blonde Lehrer das Geleite.

Des Todes reine Bilder schaun von Kirchenfenstern;
Doch wirkt ein blutiger Grund sehr trauervoll und düster.
Das Tor blieb heut verschlossen. Den Schlüssel hat der Küster.
Im Garten spricht die Schwester freundlich mit Gespenstern.

In alten Kellern reift der Wein ins Goldne, Klare.
Süß duften Äpfel. Freude glänzt nicht allzu ferne.
Den langen Abend hören Kinder Märchen gerne;
Auch zeigt sich sanftem Wahnsinn oft das Goldne, Wahre.

Das Blau fließt voll Reseden; in Zimmern Kerzenhelle.
Bescheidenen ist ihre Stätte wohl bereitet.
Den Saum des Walds hinab ein einsam Schicksal gleitet;
Die Nacht erscheint, der Ruhe Engel, auf der Schwelle.

IN EIN ALTES STAMMBUCH

Immer wieder kehrst du Melancholie,
O Sanftmut der einsamen Seele.
Zu Ende glüht ein goldener Tag.

Demutsvoll beugt sich dem Schmerz der Geduldige
Tönend von Wohllaut und weichem Wahnsinn.
Siehe! es dämmert schon.

Wieder kehrt die Nacht und klagt ein Sterbliches
Und es leidet ein anderes mit.

Schaudernd unter herbstlichen Sternen
Neigt sich jährlich tiefer das Haupt.

FOREST NOOK

To Karl Minnich

Brown chestnut trees. Gently the old folk glide
Into serener evening; softly the lovely leaves fade.
By the graveyard the blackbird jokes with my dead cousin,
The fair-haired teacher bears Angela company.

Pure images of death gaze from church windows;
Yet bloody ground appears most sorrowful and gloomy.
The gate today stayed locked. The sexton holds the key.
In the garden sister has friendly words with ghosts.

In ancient vaults wine ripens to sheer gold and clearness.
Apples smell sweet. Joy radiates not too far off.
Children love hearing fairytales the livelong evening;
What's golden, true, may often show itself to gentle madness.

Blueness is flooded with resedas; bright candlelight in rooms.
The poor in spirit have their places ready.
A lonely destiny glides down along the forest edge;
Night, the angel of repose, appears upon the threshold.

IN AN OLD FAMILY ALBUM

Ever again you return, Melancholy,
O meekness of the solitary soul.
A golden day glows and expires.

Humbly the patient man surrenders to pain
Ringing with melodious sound and soft madness.
Look! There's the twilight.

Night returns once more and a mortal thing laments
And another suffers in sympathy.

Shuddering under autumn stars
Yearly the head is bowed deeper.

MENSCHHEIT

Menschheit vor Feuerschlünden aufgestellt,
Ein Trommelwirbel, dunkler Krieger Stirnen,
Schritte durch Blutnebel; schwarzes Eisen schellt,
Verzweiflung, Nacht in traurigen Gehirnen:
Hier Evas Schatten, Jagd und rotes Geld.
Gewölk, das Licht durchbricht, das Abendmahl.
Es wohnt in Brot und Wein ein sanftes Schweigen
Und jene sind versammelt zwölf an Zahl.
Nachts schrein im Schlaf sie unter Ölbaumzweigen;
Sankt Thomas taucht die Hand ins Wundenmal.

DE PROFUNDIS

Es ist ein Stoppelfeld, in das ein schwarzer Regen fällt.
Es ist ein brauner Baum, der einsam dasteht.
Es ist ein Zischelwind, der leere Hütten umkreist.
Wie traurig dieser Abend.

Am Weiler vorbei
Sammelt die sanfte Waise noch spärliche Ähren ein.
Ihre Augen weiden rund und goldig in der Dämmerung
Und ihr Schoß harrt des himmlischen Bräutigams.

Bei der Heimkehr
Fanden die Hirten den süßen Leib
Verwest im Dornenbusch.

Ein Schatten bin ich ferne finsteren Dörfern.
Gottes Schweigen
Trank ich aus dem Brunnen des Hains.

Auf meine Stirne tritt kaltes Metall
Spinnen suchen mein Herz.
Es ist ein Licht, das in meinem Mund erlöscht.

Nachts fand ich mich auf einer Heide,
Starrend von Unrat und Staub der Sterne.
Im Haselgebüsch
Klangen wieder kristallne Engel.

MANKIND

Mankind drawn up in front of jaws of fire,
A roll of drums, dark warriors' brows,
Strides through blood-mists, black iron clashes,
Despair, night in sorrowful brains:
Eve's shadow here, pursuit and blood-red coin.
Clouds, light breaks through, the Eucharist.
In bread and wine a gentle silence dwells
And all the twelve are gathered here.
At night in sleep they cry out under olive boughs;
Saint Thomas dips his hand into the wound.

DE PROFUNDIS

There is a stubble-field into which black rain falls.
There is a brown tree standing there alone.
There is a hissing wind encircling empty huts.
What sadness in this evening.

Past the hamlet
The gentle orphan girl still garners frugal ears of corn.
Her eyes feast round and golden in the twilight
And her womb awaits the heavenly bridegroom.

Returning home
The shepherds found the sweet body
Decayed in the thorn-bush.

I am a shadow far from sombre villages.
God's silence
I drank from the spring in the grove.

Cold metal enters upon my brow,
Spiders seek out my heart.
There is a light that goes out in my mouth.

At night I found myself on a heath,
Stiff with refuse and dust of stars.
In the hazel-bush
Crystalline angels sounded again.

TROMPETEN

Unter verschnittenen Weiden, wo braune Kinder spielen
Und Blätter treiben, tönen Trompeten. Ein Kirchhofsschauer,
Fahnen von Scharlach stürzen durch des Ahorns Trauer,
Reiter entlang an Roggenfeldern, leeren Mühlen.

Oder Hirten singen nachts und Hirsche treten
In den Kreis ihrer Feuer, des Hains uralte Trauer,
Tanzende heben sich von einer schwarzen Mauer;
Fahnen von Scharlach, Lachen, Wahnsinn, Trompeten.

DIE RATTEN

In Hof scheint weiß der herbstliche Mond.
Vom Dachrand fallen phantastische Schatten.
Ein Schweigen in leeren Fenstern wohnt;
Da tauchen leise herauf die Ratten

Und huschen pfeifend hier und dort
Und ein gräulicher Dunsthauch wittert
Ihnen nach aus dem Abort,
Den geisterhaft der Mondschein durchzittert

Und sie keifen vor Gier wie toll
Und erfüllen Haus und Scheunen,
Die von Korn und Früchten voll.
Eisige Winde im Dunkel greinen.

PSALM I

Zweite Fassung

Karl Kraus zugeeignet

Es ist ein Licht, das der Wind ausgelöscht hat.
Es ist ein Heidekrug, den am Nachmittag ein Betrunkener verläßt.
Es ist ein Weinberg, verbrannt und schwarz mit Löchern voll Spinnen.
Es ist ein Raum, den sie mit Milch getüncht haben.

TRUMPETS

Under mutilated willows, where brown children play
And leaves are driven, trumpets sound. A graveyard shudder,
Scarlet banners storm through the sycamore's grief,
Horsemen past fields of rye, empty mills.

Or shepherds sing by night and stags step
Into the circle of their fires, the grove's primal grief,
Dancers arise from a black wall,
Scarlet banners, laughter, madness, trumpets.

THE RATS

Into the yard the autumn moon shines white.
From the roof's edge fantastic shadows fall,
In empty windows silence dwells;
The rats then quietly steal to the surface

And dart whistling hither and thither
And a horrid vaprous breath wafts
After them out of the sewer
Through which the ghostly moonlight trembles

And they brawl, maddened with greed
And crowd the house and barns
That are filled with corn and fruit.
Icy winds grizzle in the dark.

PSALM I

Second version
Dedicated to Karl Kraus

There is a light which the wind has extinguished.
There is a village pump which a drunk quits in the afternoon.
There is a vineyard, burnt and black, with holes full of spiders.
There is a room they have whitewashed with milk.

Der Wahnsinnige ist gestorben. Es ist eine Insel der Südsee,
Den Sonnengott zu empfangen. Man rührt die Trommeln.
Die Männer führen kriegerische Tänze auf.
Die Frauen wiegen die Hüften in Schlinggewächsen und Feuerblumen,
Wenn das Meer singt. O unser verlorenes Paradies.

Die Nymphen haben die goldenen Wälder verlassen.
Man begräbt den Fremden. Dann hebt ein Flimmerregen an.
Der Sohn des Pan erscheint in Gestalt eines Erdarbeiters,
Der den Mittag am glühenden Asphalt verschläft.
Es sind kleine Mädchen in einem Hof in Kleidchen voll herzzerreißender Armut!
Es sind Zimmer, erfüllt von Akkorden und Sonaten.
Es sind Schatten, die sich vor einem erblindeten Spiegel umarmen.
An den Fenstern des Spitals wärmen sich Genesende.
Ein weißer Dampfer am Kanal trägt blutige Seuchen herauf.

Die fremde Schwester erscheint wieder in jemands bösen Träumen.
Ruhend im Haselgebüsch spielt sie mit seinen Sternen.
Der Student, vielleicht ein Doppelgänger, schaut ihr lange vom Fenster nach.
Hinter ihm steht sein toter Bruder, oder er geht die alte Wendeltreppe herab.
Im Dunkel brauner Kastanien verblaßt die Gestalt des jungen Novizen.
Der Garten ist im Abend. Im Kreuzgang flattern die Fledermäuse umher.

Die Kinder des Hausmeisters hören zu spielen auf und suchen das Gold des
    Himmels.
Endakkorde eines Quartetts. Die kleine Blinde läuft zitternd durch die Allee,
Und später tastet ihr Schatten an kalten Mauern hin, umgeben von Märchen
    und heiligen Legenden.

Es ist ein leeres Boot, das am Abend den schwarzen Kanal heruntertreibt.
In der Düsternis des alten Asyls verfallen menschliche Ruinen.
Die toten Waisen liegen an der Gartenmauer.
Aus grauen Zimmern treten Engel mit kotgefleckten Flügeln.
Würmer tropfen von ihren vergilbten Lidern.
Der Platz vor der Kirche ist finster und schweigsam, wie in den Tagen der Kindheit.
Auf silbernen Sohlen gleiten frühere Leben vorbei
Und die Schatten der Verdammten steigen zu den seufzenden Wassern nieder.
In seinem Grab spielt der weiße Magier mit seinen Schlangen.

Schweigsam über der Schädelstätte öffnen sich Gottes goldene Augen.

The madman has died. There is a South Sea island
To receive the sungod. The drums are being beaten.
Men perform warlike dances.
Women sway their hips in creeping plants and fire flowers,
When the ocean sings. O our paradise lost.

The nymphs have deserted the golden woods.
The stranger is buried. Quivering rain begins to fall.
The son of Pan appears in the form of a labourer
Who sleeps through the midday hour on scorching asphalt.
There are little girls in the yard in dresses of heart-rending poverty!
There are rooms filled with chords and sonatas.
There are shadows that embrace before a dulled mirror.
By the hospital windows those on the way to health warm themselves.
A white steamer on the canal conveys bloody contagion.

The strange sister appears once more in someone's evil dreams.
Resting in hazel thickets she plays with his stars.
The student, perhaps a double, gazes long after her from the window.
Behind him his dead brother stands, or walks down the winding stair.
In the shade of brown chestnuts the form of the young novice pales.
The garden is in the evening. Bats flutter about in the cloisters.

The caretaker's children cease playing and look for the gold of the sky.
Final chords of a quartet. The little blind girl runs shivering down the
     avenue,
And later her shadow feels its way along cold walls, surrounded by
     fairytales and sacred legends.

There is an empty boat that at evening drifts down the black canal
In the gloom of the ancient asylum human ruins decay.
The dead orphans lie by the garden wall.
Out of the grey rooms step angels with mud-spattered wings.
Worms drip from their yellowed eyelids.
The square before the church is dark and mute, as in the days of childhood.
On silver soles former lives glide past
And the shades of the damned descend to the sighing waters.
In his grave the white magician plays with his serpents.

Silently, above the place of skulls, God's golden eyes open.

ROSENKRANZLIEDER

An die Schwester

Wo du gehst wird Herbst und Abend,
Blaues Wild, das unter Bäumen tönt,
Einsamer Weiher am Abend.

Leise der Flug der Vögel tönt,
Die Schwermut über deinen Augenbogen.
Dein schmales Lächeln tönt.

Gott hat deine Lider verbogen.
Sterne suchen nachts, Karfreitagskind,
Deinen Stirnenbogen.

NÄHE DES TODES

Zweite Fassung

O der Abend, der in die finsteren Dörfer der Kindheit geht.
Der Weiher unter den Weiden
Füllt sich mit den verpesteten Seufzern der Schwermut.

O der Wald, der leise die braunen Augen senkt,
Da aus des Einsamen knöchernen Händen
Der Purpur seiner verzückten Tage hinsinkt.

O die Nähe des Todes. Laß uns beten.
In dieser Nacht lösen auf lauen Kissen
Vergilbt von Weihrauch sich der Liebenden schmächtige Glieder.

AMEN

Verwestes gleitend durch die morsche Stube;
Schatten an gelben Tapeten; in dunklen Spiegeln wölbt
Sich unserer Hände elfenbeinerne Traurigkeit.

Braune Perlen rinnen durch die erstorbenen Finger.
In der Stille
Tun sich eines Engels blaue Mohnaugen auf.

SONGS OF THE ROSARY

To my sister

Where you walk it turns autumn and evening,
Beneath trees, blue game that sounds.
Lonely pond at eventide.

Quiet the flight of birds sounds,
Melancholy over your eyebrows.
Your slender smile sounds.

God has distorted your eyelids.
Stars seek at night, Good Friday child,
The sweep of your brow.

NEARNESS OF DEATH

Second version

O the evening which goes into the gloomy villages of childhood.
The pond beneath the willows
Is filled with the festering sighs of melancholy.

O the forest which quietly lowers its brown eyes,
When the purple of its ecstatic days
Sinks down from the bony hands of the lonely.

O nearness of death. Let us pray.
This night on mellow pillows
Yellowed with incense the lovers' slight limbs loosen.

AMEN

Corruption gliding through the rotted chamber;
Shadows on yellow wallpaper; in dark mirrors is arched
The ivory sadness of our hands.

Brown pearls trickle through the unfeeling fingers.
In the silence
The poppy blue eyes of an angel are opened.

Blau ist auch der Abend;
Die Stunde unseres Absterbens, Azraels Schatten,
Der ein braunes Gärtchen verdunkelt.

VERFALL

Am Abend, wenn die Glocken Frieden läuten,
Folg ich der Vögel wundervollen Flügen,
Die lang geschart, gleich frommen Pilgerzügen,
Entschwinden in den herbstlich klaren Weiten.

Hinwandelnd durch den dämmervollen Garten
Träum ich nach ihren helleren Geschicken
Und fühl der Stunden Weiser kaum mehr rücken.
So folg ich über Wolken ihren Fahrten.

Da macht ein Hauch mich von Verfall erzittern.
Die Amsel klagt in den entlaubten Zweigen.
Es schwankt der rote Wein an rostigen Gittern,

Indes wie blasser Kinder Todesreigen
Um dunkle Brunnenränder, die verwittern,
Im Wind sich fröstelnd blaue Astern neigen.

IM DORF

1

Aus braunen Mauern tritt ein Dorf, ein Feld.
Ein Hirt verwest auf einem alten Stein.
Der Saum des Walds schließt blaue Tiere ein,
Das sanfte Laub, das in die Stille fällt.

Der Bauern braune Stirnen. Lange tönt
Die Abendglocke; schön ist frommer Brauch,
Des Heilands schwarzes Haupt im Dornenstrauch,
Die kühle Stube, die der Tod versöhnt.

Blue also is the evening;
The hour of our dying, Azrael's shadow,
Which darkens a little brown garden.

DECAY

At evening, when the bells are tolling peace,
I follow the wondrous flights of birds,
Which gathered long like pious pilgrims' trains,
Vanish afar in autumn's clear expanses.

Meandering through the garden filled with twilight
I dream about their brighter destinies
And scarcely feel the hours' pointers move.
So follow I their paths above the clouds.

A breath of decay then makes me shudder.
The blackbird laments in leafless branches.
The red vine on the rusty railings wavers,

While like a dance of death with pallid children
Around dark rims of wells, which slowly weather,
Blue asters shivering in the wind are drooping.

IN THE VILLAGE

1

Out of brown walls a village appears, a field.
A shepherd rots upon an ancient stone.
The forest edge enfolds blue animals,
The gentle leaves that into silence fall.

Brown foreheads of the farmers. Long tolls
The evening bell; lovely is pious custom,
The Saviour's black head in a clump of thorns,
The chamber cool which death redeems.

Wie bleich die Mütter sind. Die Bläue sinkt
Auf Glas und Truh, die stolz ihr Sinn bewahrt;
Auch neigt ein weißes Haupt sich hochbejahrt
Aufs Enkelkind, das Milch und Sterne trinkt.

2

Der Arme, der im Geiste einsam starb,
Steigt wächsern über einen alten Pfad.
Die Apfelbäume sinken kahl und stad
Ins Farbige ihrer Frucht, die schwarz verdarb.

Noch immer wölbt das Dach aus dürrem Stroh
Sich übern Schlaf der Kühe. Die blinde Magd
Erscheint im Hof; ein blaues Wasser klagt;
Ein Pferdeschädel starrt vom morschen Tor.

Der Idiot spricht dunklen Sinns ein Wort
Der Liebe, das im schwarzen Busch verhallt,
Wo jene steht in schmaler Traumgestalt.
Der Abend tönt in feuchter Bläue fort.

3

Ans Fenster schlagen Äste föhnentlaubt.
Im Schoß der Bäurin wächst ein wildes Weh.
Durch ihre Arme rieselt schwarzer Schnee;
Goldäugige Eulen flattern um ihr Haupt.

Die Mauern starren kahl und grauverdreckt
Ins kühle Dunkel. Im Fieberbette friert
Der schwangere Leib, den frech der Mond bestiert.
Vor ihrer Kammer ist ein Hund verreckt.

Drei Männer treten finster durch das Tor
Mit Sensen, die im Feld zerbrochen sind.
Durchs Fenster klirrt der rote Abendwind;
Ein schwarzer Engel tritt daraus hervor.

How pale the mothers are. Blueness sinks down
On glass and chest cherished by their proud sense;
And a white head advanced in years stoops low
To grandchild which drinks milk and stars.

2

The poor man who in spirit lonely died,
Climbs waxen up an ancient path.
The apple trees sink bare and still
Into the colour of their fruit, which then turned black.

The roof of paltry straw still arches
Over the sleep of cows. The blind milkmaid
Appears in the yard; blue water that laments;
A horse's skull stares from a rotten gate.

The idiot with dark meaning speaks a word
Of love which dies away in the black bush,
Where she does stand in slender shape of dream,
The evening in moist blueness still rings on.

3

Branches flay windows stripped by the southern breeze.
In the peasant woman's womb there grows a savage pang.
Through her arms trickles black snow;
Golden-eyed owls flutter about her head.

The walls stare barren and besmirched with grey
Into cool darkness. In fevered bed freezes
The pregnant body, brazenly ogled by the moon.
Before her chamber a dog has breathed his wretched last.

Three men step darkly through the gate
With scythes that have been broken in the field.
Through window rattles the red evening wind;
A black angel out of it appears.

ABENDLIED

Am Abend, wenn wir auf dunklen Pfaden gehn,
Erscheinen unsere bleichen Gestalten vor uns.

Wenn uns dürstet,
Trinken wir die weißen Wasser des Teichs,
Die Süße unserer traurigen Kindheit.

Erstorbene ruhen wir unterm Hollundergebüsch,
Schaun den grauen Möven zu.

Frühlingsgewölke steigen über die finstere Stadt,
Die der Mönche edlere Zeiten schweigt.

Da ich deine schmalen Hände nahm
Schlugst du leise die runden Augen auf,
Dieses ist lange her.

Doch wenn dunkler Wohllaut die Seele heimsucht,
Erscheinst du Weiße in des Freundes herbstlicher Landschaft.

DREI BLICKE IN EINEN OPAL

An Erhard Buschbeck

1

Blick in Opal: ein Dorf umkränzt von dürrem Wein,
Der Stille grauer Wolken, gelber Felsenhügel
Und abendlicher Quellen Kühle: Zwillingsspiegel
Umrahmt von Schatten und von schleimigem Gestein.

Des Herbstes Weg und Kreuze gehn in Abend ein,
Singende Pilger und die blutbefleckten Linnen.
Des Einsamen Gestalt kehrt also sich nach innen
Und geht, ein bleicher Engel, durch den leeren Hain.

Aus Schwarzem bläst der Föhn. Mit Satyrn im Verein
Sind schlanke Weiblein; Mönche der Wollust bleiche Priester,
Ihr Wahnsinn schmückt mit Lilien sich schön und düster
Und hebt die Hände auf zu Gottes goldenem Schrein.

EVENING SONG

At evening, when we walk along dark paths,
Our pale figures appear before us.

When we thirst,
We drink the white waters of the pool,
The sweetness of our sad childhood.

Deceased, we rest beneath elder bushes,
Gaze on the grey gulls.

Spring clouds rise above the gloomy town
Which holds its peace on the monks' nobler times.

When I took your slender hands,
You gently looked up with round eyes.
This is long past.

Yet when dark harmony seeks out the soul,
You, white one, appear in your friend's autumn landscape.

THREE GLANCES INTO AN OPAL

To Erhard Buschbeck

1

Glance into opal: a village wreathed in arid vines,
The silence of grey clouds, of yellow rocky hills
And coolness of evening springs: twin mirrors
Framed by shadows and by slimy stones.

Autumn's path and crosses merge into evening,
Singing pilgrims and blood-stained linen.
The form of the lonely man thus turns inwards
And walks, a pale angel, through the empty grove.

The southern breeze blows out of blackness. Slender young wenches
Consort with satyrs; monks of lechery pale priests,
Their madness adorns itself with lilies lovely and sombre
And raises hands to God's golden shrine.

Der ihn befeuchtet, rosig hängt ein Tropfen Tau
Im Rosmarin: hinfließt ein Hauch von Grabgerüchen,
Spitälern, wirr erfüllt von Fieberschrein und Flüchen.
Gebein steigt aus dem Erbbegräbnis morsch und grau.

In blauem Schleim und Schleiern tanzt des Greisen Frau,
Das schmutzstarrende Haar erfüllt von schwarzen Tränen,
Die Knaben träumen wirr in dürren Weidensträhnen
Und ihre Stirnen sind von Aussatz kahl und rauh.

Durchs Bogenfenster sinkt ein Abend lind und lau.
Ein Heiliger tritt aus seinen schwarzen Wundenmalen.
Die Purpurschnecken kriechen aus zerbrochenen Schalen
Und speien Blut in Dorngewinde starr und grau.

Die Blinden streuen in eiternde Wunden Weiherauch.
Rotgoldene Gewänder; Fackeln; Psalmensingen;
Und Mädchen, die wie Gift den Leib des Herrn umschlingen.
Gestalten schreiten wächsernstarr durch Glut und Rauch.

Aussätziger mitternächtigen Tanz führt an ein Gauch
Dürrknöchern. Garten wunderlicher Abenteuer;
Verzerrtes; Blumenfratzen, Lachen; Ungeheuer
Und rollendes Gestirn im schwarzen Dornenstrauch.

O Armut, Bettelsuppe, Brot und süßer Lauch;
Des Lebens Träumerei in Hütten vor den Wäldern.
Grau härtet sich der Himmel über gelben Feldern
Und eine Abendglocke singt nach altem Brauch.

2

A dewdrop that moistens it hangs rose-coloured
In rosemary: a breath of graveyard odours oozes out,
To hospitals filled with a maze of fever-cries and curses.
Bones rise from ancestral burial putrid and grey.

In blue slime and veils the old man's wife dances,
Her muck-stiffened hair filled with black tears,
Young boys dream wildly in thin willow-strands,
And their brows are bald and coarse with leprosy.

Through the arched window an evening sinks gentle and mild.
A saint steps out of his wounds' black marks.
The crimson snails crawl out of broken shells
And spew blood into twisted thorns stiff and grey.

3

The blind strew incense into festering wounds.
Red gold attire; torches; psalms intoned;
And girls who embrace the body of Our Lord like poison.
Figures stride with waxen stiffness through heat and smoke.

Midnight dance of lepers is led by a fool
Dry-boned. Gardens of strange adventure;
Distortions; grimacing flowers, laughter; monsters
And revolving stars in the black thornbush.

O poverty, beggars' broth, bread and sweet leeks;
Life's reverie in huts by the forest.
The sky hardens grey above yellow fields
And an evening bell sings after ancient custom.

NACHTLIED

Des Unbewegten Odem. Ein Tiergesicht
Erstarrt vor Bläue, ihrer Heiligkeit.
Gewaltig ist das Schweigen im Stein;

Die Maske eines nächtlichen Vogels. Sanfter Dreiklang
Verklingt in einem. Elai! dein Antlitz
Beugt sich sprachlos über bläuliche Wasser.

O! ihr stillen Spiegel der Wahrheit.
An des Einsamen elfenbeinerner Schläfe
Erscheint der Abglanz gefallener Engel.

HELIAN

In den einsamen Stunden des Geistes
Ist es schön, in der Sonne zu gehn
An den gelben Mauern des Sommers hin.
Leise klingen die Schritte im Gras; doch immer schläft
Der Sohn des Pan im grauen Marmor.

Abends auf der Terrasse betranken wir uns mit braunem Wein.
Rötlich glüht der Pfirsich im Laub;
Sanfte Sonate, frohes Lachen.

Schön ist die Stille der Nacht.
Auf dunklem Plan
Begegnen wir uns mit Hirten und weißen Sternen.

Wenn es Herbst geworden ist
Zeigt sich nüchterne Klarheit im Hain.
Besänftigte wandeln wir an roten Mauern hin
Und die runden Augen folgen dem Flug der Vögel.
Am Abend sinkt das weiße Wasser in Graburnen.

In kahlen Gezweigen feiert der Himmel.
In reinen Händen trägt der Landmann Brot und Wein
Und friedlich reifen die Früchte in sonniger Kammer.

The breath of the unmoved. The face of an animal
Stiffens with blueness, of her sacredness.
Mighty is the silence in stone;

The mask of a bird of night. Gentle triad
Dies away within one. Elai! Your countenance
Bends speechless over bluish waters.

O! You silent mirrors of truth.
On the ivory brow of the lonely
Appears the reflected glory of fallen angels.

In solitary hours of the mind
It is lovely to walk in the sun
Passing along the yellow walls of summer.
Our soft footfall rings in the grass; yet the Son of Pan
For ever sleeps in grey marble.

At evening on the terrace we grew besotted with brown wine.
The peach glows reddish among leaves;
Gentle sonata; joyous laughter.

Lovely is the stillness of night.
On the dark plain
We meet with shepherds and white stars.

When autumn has come
Piercing lucidity gleams in the grove.
Soothed we meander along red walls
And our round eyes follow the flight of birds.
At eventide white water sinks into burial urns.

In bare branches the sky is jubilant.
In his pure hands the countryman bears bread and wine
And fruits of the field show tranquil ripeness in sunlit chamber.

O wie ernst ist das Antlitz der teueren Toten.
Doch die Seele erfreut gerechtes Anschaun.

Gewaltig ist das Schweigen des verwüsteten Gartens,
Da der junge Novize die Stirne mit braunem Laub bekränzt,
Sein Odem eisiges Gold trinkt.

Die Hände rühren das Alter bläulicher Wasser
Oder in kalter Nacht die weißen Wangen der Schwestern.

Leise und harmonisch ist ein Gang an freundlichen Zimmern hin,
Wo Einsamkeit ist und das Rauschen des Ahorns,
Wo vielleicht noch die Drossel singt.

Schön ist der Mensch und erscheinend im Dunkel,
Wenn er staunend Arme und Beine bewegt,
Und in purpurnen Höhlen stille die Augen rollen.

Zur Vesper verliert sich der Fremdling in schwarzer Novemberzerstörung,
Unter morschem Geäst, an Mauern voll Aussatz hin,
Wo vordem der heilige Bruder gegangen,
Versunken in das sanfte Saitenspiel seines Wahnsinns,

O wie einsam endet der Abendwind.
Ersterbend neigt sich das Haupt im Dunkel des Ölbaums.

Erschütternd ist der Untergang des Geschlechts.
In dieser Stunde füllen sich die Augen des Schauenden
Mit dem Gold seiner Sterne.

Am Abend versinkt ein Glockenspiel, das nicht mehr tönt,
Verfallen die schwarzen Mauern am Platz,
Ruft der tote Soldat zum Gebet.

Ein bleicher Engel
Tritt der Sohn ins leere Haus seiner Väter.

Die Schwestern sind ferne zu weißen Greisen gegangen.
Nachts fand sie der Schläfer unter den Säulen im Hausflur,
Zurückgekehrt von traurigen Pilgerschaften.

O how grave is the countenance of those dear ones deceased.
Yet the soul is gladdened by righteous contemplation.

Mighty is the silence of the desolate garden,
When the young novice wreathes his brow with brown leaves,
His breath drinks in icy gold.

Hands that touch the age of bluish waters
Or in the chill night the white cheeks of his sisters.

A stroll past welcoming rooms is quiet and harmonious,
Where solitude is and the stir of the sycamore tree,
Where perhaps the thrush is singing still.

Lovely is Man and appearing in darkness,
When astounded he sets arms and legs in motion,
And his tranquil eyes roll in crimson hollows.

At supper the stranger is lost in the black ruin of November,
Under rotting branches, passing walls filled with pestilence,
Where the saintly brother had earlier walked,
Lost in the gentle string playing of his madness,

O how lonely is the ending of the evening breeze.
In death the head is inclined in the darkness of the olive tree.

Shattering is the decline of our race.
At this hour the eyes of the gazer are filled
With the gold of his stars.

At evening a carillon that chimes no more dies away,
Ruined are the black walls by the square,
The dead soldier calls to prayer.

A pallid angel
The son steps into the empty house of his fathers.

The sisters have gone far away to white old men.
At night the sleeper found them among the pillars of the hall,
Returned from sad pilgrimages.

O wie starrt von Kot und Würmern ihr Haar,
Da er darein mit silbernen Füßen steht,
Und jene verstorben aus kahlen Zimmern treten.

O ihr Psalmen in feurigen Mitternachtsregen,
Da die Knechte mit Nesseln die sanften Augen schlugen,
Die kindlichen Früchte des Hollunders
Sich staunend neigen über ein leeres Grab.

Leise rollen vergilbte Monde
Über die Fieberlinnen des Jünglings,
Eh dem Schweigen des Winters folgt.

Ein erhabenes Schicksal sinnt den Kidron hinab,
Wo die Zeder, ein weiches Geschöpf,
Sich unter den blauen Brauen des Vaters entfaltet,
Über die Weide nachts ein Schäfer seine Herde führt.
Oder es sind Schreie im Schlaf,
Wenn ein eherner Engel im Hain den Menschen antritt,
Das Fleisch des Heiligen auf glühendem Rost hinschmilzt.

Um die Lehmhütten rankt purpurner Wein,
Tönende Bündel vergilbten Korns,
Das Summen der Bienen, der Flug des Kranichs.
Am Abend begegnen sich Auferstandene auf Felsenpfaden.

In schwarzen Wassern spiegeln sich Aussätzige;
Oder sie öffnen die kotbefleckten Gewänder
Weinend dem balsamischen Wind, der vom rosigen Hügel weht.

Schlanke Mägde tasten durch die Gassen der Nacht,
Ob sie den liebenden Hirten fänden.
Sonnabends tönt in den Hütten sanfter Gesang.

Lasset das Lied auch des Knaben gedenken,
Seines Wahnsinns, und weißer Brauen und seines Hingangs,
Des Verwesten, der bläulich die Augen aufschlägt.
O wie traurig ist dieses Wiedersehn.

O how stiff with muck and worms is their hair,
Wherein with silver feet he stands,
And those deceased enter from barren rooms.

O you psalms in fiery midnight rain,
When the servants beat those gentle eyes with nettles,
The childlike fruits of the elder-bush
Droop astounded over an empty tomb.

Yellowed moons roll in silence
Above the youth's fever-linen,
Ere yet the silence of winter follows.

A sublime destiny is pondered down along Cedron,
Where the cedar, a tender creature,
Unfolds beneath the blue brow of the father,
Over the pasture by night a shepherd leads his flock.
Or there are cries in sleep,
When a brazen angel meets with Man in the grove,
The flesh of the saint melts away on a glowing grill.

Crimson vines entwine about huts of clay,
Sounding sheafs of yellow corn,
The humming of bees, the flight of the crane.
At eventide the resurrected meet on stony paths.

In black waters lepers are mirrored;
Or they open their muck-stained raiment
Weeping to the fragrant wind wafted from the rosy hill.

Slender maids grope through alleys of the night,
Might they not find the loving shepherd.
On Sabbath eve soft singing sounds in the huts.

Let your song also remember the youth,
His madness, his white brow and his departing,
The one now decayed whose eyes open their blueness.
O how sad is this reunion.

Die Stufen des Wahnsinns in schwarzen Zimmern,
Die Schatten der Alten unter der offenen Tür,
Da Helians Seele sich im rosigen Spiegel beschaut
Und Schnee und Aussatz von seiner Stirne sinken.

An den Wänden sind die Sterne erloschen
Und die weißen Gestalten des Lichts.

Dem Teppich entsteigt Gebein der Gräber,
Das Schweigen verfallener Kreuze am Hügel,
Des Weihrauchs Süße im purpurnen Nachtwind.

O ihr zerbrochenen Augen in schwarzen Mündern,
Da der Enkel in sanfter Umnachtung
Einsam dem dunkleren Ende nachsinnt,
Der stille Gott die blauen Lider über ihn senkt.

The stages of madness in black rooms,
The shades of the ancient beneath the open door,
When Helian's soul surveys itself in the rosy glass
And snow and leprosy fall away from his brow.

By the walls the stars have gone out
And the white figures of light.

From the carpet there rise the bones of the buried,
The silence of crosses decayed on the hill,
The sweetness of incense in the crimson wind of night.

O you broken eyes in black mouths,
When the grandchild in gentle derangement
Ponders the darker ending in solitude,
The silent god lowers blue eyelids upon him.

KINDHEIT

Voll Früchten der Hollunder; ruhig wohnte die Kindheit
In blauer Höhle. Über vergangenen Pfad,
Wo nun bräunlich das wilde Gras saust,
Sinnt das stille Geäst; das Rauschen des Laubs

Ein gleiches, wenn das blaue Wasser im Felsen tönt.
Sanft ist der Amsel Klage. Ein Hirt
Folgt sprachlos der Sonne, die vom herbstlichen Hügel rollt.

Ein blauer Augenblick ist nur mehr Seele.
Am Waldsaum zeigt sich ein scheues Wild und friedlich
Ruhn im Grund die alten Glocken und finsteren Weiler.

Frömmer kennst du den Sinn der dunklen Jahre,
Kühle und Herbst in einsamen Zimmern;
Und in heiliger Bläue läuten leuchtende Schritte fort.

Leise klirrt ein offenes Fenster; zu Tränen
Rührt der Anblick des verfallenen Friedhofs am Hügel,
Erinnerung an erzählte Legenden; doch manchmal erhellt sich die Seele,
Wenn sie frohe Menschen denkt, dunkelgoldene Frühlingstage.

STUNDENLIED

Mit dunklen Blicken sehen sich die Liebenden an,
Die Blonden, Strahlenden. In starrender Finsternis
Umschlingen schmächtig sich die sehnenden Arme.

Purpurn zerbrach der Gesegneten Mund. Die runden Augen
Spiegeln das dunkle Gold des Frühlingsnachmittags,
Saum und Schwärze des Walds, Abendängste im Grün;
Vielleicht unsäglichen Vogelflug, des Ungeborenen

CHILDHOOD

Full of fruit the elder bush; childhood dwelt tranquil
In a blue cave. Above the path of traversed time,
Where brownish the wild grass now whistles,
Silent branches ponder; the rustle of foliage

Alike, when the blue water rings in the rock.
Gentle is the blackbird's lament. A shepherd
Follows the sun speechless, which rolls from the autumn hill.

A blue moment is nothing but soul.
By the forest's edge shy game appears and peaceful
The ancient bells and gloomy hamlets rest in the valley.

More pious, you know the meaning of the dark years,
Coolness and autumn in lonely rooms;
And in sacred blueness shining steps ring on.

An open window quietly rattles; the sight of
The ruined graveyard by the hill moves to tears,
Recollection of legends told; yet sometimes the soul brightens
When it ponders joyful people, dark golden days in spring.

SONG OF HOURS

With dark glances the lovers gaze at each other,
The blond, the radiant. In frozen darkness
Yearning arms in fragile embrace.

Crimson the mouth of the expectant woman broke. The round eyes
Mirror the dark gold of the spring afternoon,
Border and blackness of the forest, evening fears amidst greenery,
Perhaps ineffable bird flight, the path of the unborn

Pfad an finsteren Dörfern, einsamen Sommern hin
Und aus verfallener Bläue tritt bisweilen ein Abgelebtes.

Leise rauscht im Acker das gelbe Korn.
Hart ist das Leben und stählern schwingt die Sense der Landmann,
Fügt gewaltige Balken der Zimmermann.

Purpurn färbt sich das Laub im Herbst; der mönchische Geist
Durchwandelt heitere Tage; reif ist die Traube
Und festlich die Luft in geräumigen Höfen.
Süßer duften vergilbte Früchte; leise ist das Lachen
Des Frohen, Musik und Tanz in schattigen Kellern;
Im dämmernden Garten Schritt und Stille des verstorbenen Knaben.

UNTERWEGS

Am Abend trugen sie den Fremden in die Totenkammer;
Ein Duft von Teer; das leise Rauschen roter Platanen;
Der dunkle Flug der Dohlen; am Platz zog eine Wache auf.
Die Sonne ist in schwarze Linnen gesunken; immer wieder kehrt dieser vergangene
    Abend.
Im Nebenzimmer spielt die Schwester eine Sonate von Schubert.
Sehr leise sinkt ihr Lächeln in den verfallenen Brunnen,
Der bläulich in der Dämmerung rauscht. O, wie alt ist unser Geschlecht.
Jemand flüstert drunten im Garten; jemand hat diesen schwarzen Himmel verlassen.
Auf der Kommode duften Äpfel. Großmutter zündet goldene Kerzen an.

O, wie mild ist der Herbst. Leise klingen unsere Schritte im alten Park
Unter hohen Bäumen. O, wie ernst ist das hyazinthene Antlitz der Dämmerung.
Der blaue Quell zu deinen Füßen, geheimnisvoll die rote Stille deines Munds,
Umdüstert vom Schlummer des Laubs, dem dunklen Gold verfallener Sonnenblumen.
Deine Lider sind schwer von Mohn und träumen leise auf meiner Stirne.
Sanfte Glocken durchzittern die Brust. Eine blaue Wolke
Ist dein Antlitz auf mich gesunken in der Dämmerung.

Ein Lied zur Guitarre, das in einer fremden Schenke erklingt,
Die wilden Hollunderbüsche dort, ein lang vergangener Novembertag,
Vertraute Schritte auf der dämmernden Stiege, der Anblick gebräunter Balken,
Ein offenes Fenster, an dem ein süßes Hoffen zurückblieb –
Unsäglich ist das alles, o Gott, daß man erschüttert ins Knie bricht.

Along dark villages, through lonely summers
And out of decayed blueness a thing deceased at times emerges.

Quietly the yellow corn rustles in the field.
Hard is life and steely the countryman swings his scythe,
Mighty beams are joined by the carpenter.

Crimson the leaves colour in autumn; the monastic spirit
Passes through cheerful days; ripe is the grape
And festive the air in spacious farmsteads.
Sweeter the smell of faded fruit; quiet is the laughter
Of the cheerful, music and dancing in shady cellars;
In the twilit garden the footfall and silence of the young boy who died.

ON A JOURNEY

At evening they bore the stranger into the death-chamber;
A sweet smell of tar; the soft rustling of red plane trees;
The dark flight of jackdaws; on the square a guard was mounted.
The sun has sunk into black linen; this past evening evermore returns.
In the next room sister plays a sonata by Schubert.
Her smile sinks most gently into the ruined well
Which murmurs bluish in the twilight. O, how ancient is our race.
Someone whispers below in the garden; someone has deserted this black sky.
On the sideboard apples smell sweetly; grandmother lights golden candles.

O, how mild is the autumn. Our steps sound softly in the old park
Beneath high trees. O, how grave is the hyacinth face of twilight.
The blue source at your feet, how mysterious the red silence of your mouth,
Encircled by the gloom of slumbering leaves, the dark gold of decaying
    sunflowers.
Your eyelids are heavy with poppyseed and gently dream on my brow.
Gentle bells tremble through the breast. A blue cloud,
Your face has sunk down on me in the twilight.

A song for guitar struck up in a strange tavern,
The wild elder-bushes there, a November day long past,
Familiar steps on the twilit stair, the sight of beams turned brown,
An open window where a sweet hope lingered –
All this, O God, is so unutterable that one falls shattered to one's knees.

O, wie dunkel ist diese Nacht. Eine purpurne Flamme
Erlosch an meinem Mund. In der Stille
Erstirbt der bangen Seele einsames Saitenspiel.
Laß, wenn trunken von Wein das Haupt in die Gosse sinkt.

LANDSCHAFT

Zweite Fassung

Septemberabend; traurig tönen die dunklen Rufe der Hirten
Durch das dämmernde Dorf; Feuer sprüht in der Schmiede.
Gewaltig bäumt sich ein schwarzes Pferd; die hyazinthenen Locken der Magd
Haschen nach der Inbrunst seiner purpurnen Nüstern.
Leise erstarrt am Saum des Waldes der Schrei der Hirschkuh
Und die gelben Blumen des Herbstes
Neigen sich sprachlos über das blaue Antlitz des Teichs.
In roter Flamme verbrannte ein Baum; aufflattern mit dunklen Gesichtern
    die Fledermäuse.

AN DEN KNABEN ELIS

Elis, wenn die Amsel im schwarzen Wald ruft,
Dieses ist dein Untergang.
Deine Lippen trinken die Kühle des blauen Felsenquells.

Laß, wenn deine Stirne leise blutet
Uralte Legenden
Und dunkle Deutung des Vogelflugs.

Du aber gehst mit weichen Schritten in die Nacht,
Die voll purpurner Trauben hängt,
Und du regst die Arme schöner im Blau.

Ein Dornenbusch tönt,
Wo deine mondenen Augen sind.
O, wie lange bist, Elis, du verstorben.

Dein Leib ist eine Hyazinthe,
In die ein Mönch die wachsernen Finger taucht.
Eine schwarze Höhle ist unser Schweigen,

O, how dark is this night. A crimson flame
Died in my mouth. In the silence
The lone stringed music of the fearful soul dies away.
Stay, when drunk with wine, your head sinks to the gutter.

LANDSCAPE

Second version

September evening; the dark calls of the shepherds sound sadly
Through the dwindling light of the village; fire spits sparks in the smithy.
Powerfully a black horse rears; the hyacinth locks of the maid
Clutch at the ardour of his crimson nostrils.
By the forest edge the cry of the hind quietly freezes
And the yellow flowers of autumn
Droop speechless over the blue lake's countenance.
A tree was burnt away in a red flame; bats with dark faces fly up in
    a flurry.

TO THE BOY ELIS

Elis, when the blackbird calls from the black woods,
That is your perdition.
Your lips drink in the coolness of the blue rock spring.

Leave be, when your brow quietly bleeds
Ancient legends
And dark deciphering of birdflight.

Yet you walk with gentle step into the night,
Which hangs full of purple grapes
And you move your arms lovelier in blueness.

A thorn bush sounds,
Where your moonlight eyes are.
O, how long, Elis, have you been dead.

Your body is a hyacinth
Into which a monk dips his waxen fingers.
Our silence is a black cavern,

Daraus bisweilen ein sanftes Tier tritt
Und langsam die schweren Lider senkt.
Auf deine Schläfen tropft schwarzer Tau,

Das letzte Gold verfallener Sterne.

ELIS

Dritte Fassung

1

Vollkommen ist die Stille dieses goldenen Tags.
Unter alten Eichen
Erscheinst du, Elis, ein Ruhender mit runden Augen.

Ihre Bläue spiegelt den Schlummer der Liebenden.
An deinem Mund
Verstummten ihre rosigen Seufzer.

Am Abend zog der Fischer die schweren Netze ein.
Ein guter Hirt
Führt seine Herde am Waldsaum hin,
O! wie gerecht sind, Elis, alle deine Tage.

Leise sinkt
An kahlen Mauern des Ölbaums blaue Stille,
Erstirbt eines Greisen dunkler Gesang.

Ein goldener Kahn
Schaukelt, Elis, dein Herz am einsamen Himmel.

2

Ein sanftes Glockenspiel tönt in Elis' Brust
Am Abend,
Da sein Haupt ins schwarze Kissen sinkt.

Ein blaues Wild
Blutet leise im Dorngestrüpp.

Ein brauner Baum steht abgeschieden da;
Seine blauen Früchte fielen von ihm.

From which at times a gentle animal appears
And slowly shuts its heavy eyelids.
Onto your temples black dew drips,

The final gold of vanished stars.

ELIS

Third version

1

Perfection lies in the stillness of this golden day.
Under ancient oaks
You, Elis, appear as one in repose with round eyes.

In their blueness is mirrored the slumber of lovers.
Near your mouth
Their rosy sighs fell silent.

In the evening the fisherman drew in his heavy nets.
A good shepherd
Leads his flock by the forest edge.
O! How just, Elis, are all your days.

By naked walls
Quietly descends blue stillness of the olive tree,
An old man's dark song dies away.

A golden boat,
Your heart, Elis, sways by the lonely sky.

2

A gentle chiming of bells rings in Elis's breast
In the evening,
When his head sinks into the black pillow.

A blue prey
Quietly bleeds in a thicket of thorns.

A brown tree stands there in solitude;
Its blue fruit fell away.

Zeichen und Sterne
Versinken leise im Abendweiher.

Hinter dem Hügel ist es Winter geworden.

Blaue Tauben
Trinken nachts den eisigen Schweiß,
Der von Elis' kristallener Stirne rinnt.

Immer tönt
An schwarzen Mauern Gottes einsamer Wind.

HOHENBURG

Zweite Fassung

Es ist niemand im Haus. Herbst in Zimmern;
Mondeshelle Sonate
Und das Erwachen am Saum des dämmernden Walds.

Immer denkst du das weiße Antlitz des Menschen
Ferne dem Getümmel der Zeit;
Über ein Träumendes neigt sich gerne grünes Gezweig,

Kreuz und Abend;
Umfängt den Tönenden mit purpurnen Armen sein Stern,
Der zu unbewohnten Fenstern hinaufsteigt.

Also zittert im Dunkel der Fremdling,
Da er leise die Lider über ein Menschliches aufhebt,
Das ferne ist; die Silberstimme des Windes im Hausflur.

Signs and stars
Sink and silently vanish in the evening pond.

Behind the hill winter has come.

Blue doves
Nightly drink the icy sweat
That runs off Elis's crystalline brow.

By black walls
For ever resounds God's solitary wind.

HOHENBURG

Second version

There is no one in the house. Autumn in rooms,
Moon-bright sonata
And the awakening by the edge of the twilit wood.

You ever think on man's white countenance
Removed from the turbulence of the times;
Green branches gladly bend over that which dreams,

Cross and eventide;
He who sounds aloud is embraced with crimson arms by his star
Which rises to uninhabited windows above.

Thus shudders the stranger in darkness,
As softly he raises his eyelids over a human thing
Afar off; the silver voice of the wind in the hallway.

SEBASTIAN IM TRAUM

Für Adolf Loos

1

Mutter trug das Kindlein im weißen Mond,
Im Schatten des Nußbaums, uralten Hollunders,
Trunken vom Safte des Mohns, der Klage der Drossel;
Und stille
Neigte in Mitleid sich über jene ein bärtiges Antlitz

Leise im Dunkel des Fensters; und altes Hausgerät
Der Väter
Lag im Verfall; Liebe und herbstliche Träumerei.

Also dunkel der Tag des Jahrs, traurige Kindheit,
Da der Knabe leise zu kühlen Wassern, silbernen Fischen hinabstieg,
Ruh und Antlitz;
Da er steinern sich vor rasende Rappen warf,
In grauer Nacht sein Stern über ihn kam;

Oder wenn er an der frierenden Hand der Mutter
Abends über Sankt Peters herbstlichen Friedhof ging,
Ein zarter Leichnam stille im Dunkel der Kammer lag
Und jener die kalten Lider über ihn aufhob.

Er aber war ein kleiner Vogel im kahlen Geäst,
Die Glocke lang im Abendnovember,
Des Vaters Stille, da er im Schlaf die dämmernde Wendeltreppe hinabstieg.

2

Frieden der Seele. Einsamer Winterabend,
Die dunklen Gestalten der Hirten am alten Weiher;
Kindlein in der Hütte von Stroh; o wie leise
Sank in schwarzem Fieber das Antlitz hin.
Heilige Nacht.

Oder wenn er an der harten Hand des Vaters
Stille den finstern Kalvarienberg hinanstieg
Und in dämmernden Felsennischen
Die blaue Gestalt des Menschen durch seine Legende ging,

SEBASTIAN IN A DREAM

For Adolf Loos

1

Mother carried the little child in the white moon,
In the shade of the nut-tree, of the ancient elder-bush,
Drunk with the juice of poppies, with lament of the thrush;
And silent
in pity a bearded countenance bent over the woman

Quiet in the window's darkness; and ancient chattels
Of our forefathers
Lay in decay; love and autumnal reverie.

So dark was the day of the year, a sad childhood,
When the boy stole softly down to cool waters, silver fishes,
Repose and countenance;
When stone-like he cast himself under raging black horses,
His star rose within him in greyness of night;

Or when held by his mother's chill hand
He walked at eventide over St Peter's autumn churchyard,
A gentle body lay dead in the dark of the chamber
And that man raised his cold eyelids above him.

Yet he was a little bird amid the bare branches,
The live-long bell in evening-November,
His father's silence, when in sleep he descended the twilit winding stair.

2

Peace to the soul. Lonely evening in winter,
The dark figures of shepherds by the ancient pond;
Babe in a hut of straw; O how silently
That countenance fell away in black fever.
Holy night.

Or when held by the hard hand of his father
Silent he climbed up sombre Mount Calvary
And in twilit recesses of rock
The blue figure of Man passed through his legend,

Aus der Wunde unter dem Herzen purpurn das Blut rann.
O wie leise stand in dunkler Seele das Kreuz auf.

Liebe; da in schwarzen Winkeln der Schnee schmolz,
Ein blaues Lüftchen sich heiter im alten Hollunder fing,
In dem Schattengewölbe des Nußbaums;
Und dem Knaben leise sein rosiger Engel erschien.

Freude; da in kühlen Zimmern eine Abendsonate erklang,
Im braunen Holzgebälk
Ein blauer Falter aus der silbernen Puppe kroch.

O die Nähe des Todes. In steinerner Mauer
Neigte sich ein gelbes Haupt, schweigend das Kind,
Da in jenem März der Mond verfiel.

3

Rosige Osterglocke im Grabgewölbe der Nacht
Und die Silberstimmen der Sterne,
Daß in Schauern ein dunkler Wahnsinn von der Stirne des Schläfers sank.

O wie stille ein Gang den blauen Fluß hinab
Vergessenes sinnend, da im grünen Geäst
Die Drossel ein Fremdes in den Untergang rief.

Oder wenn er an der knöchernen Hand des Greisen
Abends vor die verfallene Mauer der Stadt ging
Und jener in schwarzem Mantel ein rosiges Kindlein trug,
Im Schatten des Nußbaums der Geist des Bösen erschien.

Tasten über die grünen Stufen des Sommers. O wie leise
Verfiel der Garten in der braunen Stille des Herbstes,
Duft und Schwermut des alten Hollunders,
Da in Sebastians Schatten die Silberstimme des Engels erstarb.

From the wound under the heart the crimson blood ran.
O how gently arose in the darkness of soul the Cross.

Love; when in black corners the snow was melting,
A blue breeze was caught up brightly in the ancient elder-bush,
In the shadowy vault of the nut-tree;
And to the boy appeared quietly his rosy angel.

Joy; when in cool rooms an evening sonata was intoned,
Among rafters grown brown
A blue moth slipped from its silver chrysalis.

O the nearness of death. In a stony wall
A yellow head was bowed, the child lay in silence,
When in that March the moon decayed.

3

Rosy Easter daffodil in the grave-vault of night
And the silver voices of stars
That dark madness shuddering fell from the brow of the sleeper.

O how tranquil to walk down by the blue river
Pondering what memory has lost, when in greenest branches
The thrush called a strange thing to its ruin.

Or when held by the bony hand of the old man
At evening he went out to the ruined wall of the city
And that man bore a rosy child in his black cloak,
In the shade of the nut-tree the spirit of evil appeared.

To feel over the green stages of summer. O how gently
The garden decayed in the brown stillness of autumn,
Fragrance and melancholy of the ancient elder-tree,
When in Sebastian's shadow the angel's silver voice died away.

AM MOOR

Dritte Fassung

Wanderer im schwarzen Wind; leise flüstert das dürre Rohr
In der Stille des Moors. Am grauen Himmel
Ein Zug von wilden Vögeln folgt;
Quere über finsteren Wassern.

Aufruhr. In verfallener Hütte
Aufflattert mit schwarzen Flügeln die Fäulnis;
Verkrüppelte Birken seufzen im Wind.

Abend in verlassener Schenke. Den Heimweg umwittert
Die sanfte Schwermut grasender Herden,
Erscheinung der Nacht: Kröten tauchen aus silbernen Wassern.

IM FRÜHLING

Leise sank von dunklen Schritten der Schnee,
Im Schatten des Baums
Heben die rosigen Lider Liebende.

Immer folgt den dunklen Rufen der Schiffer
Stern und Nacht;
Und die Ruder schlagen leise im Takt.

Balde an verfallener Mauer blühen
Die Veilchen,
Ergrünt so stille die Schläfe des Einsamen.

ABEND IN LANS

Zweite Fassung

Wanderschaft durch dämmernden Sommer
An Bündeln vergilbten Korns vorbei. Unter getünchten Bogen,
Wo die Schwalbe aus und ein flog, tranken wir feurigen Wein.

Schön: o Schwermut und purpurnes Lachen.
Abend und die dunklen Düfte des Grüns
Kühlen mit Schauern die glühende Stirne uns.

BY THE MOOR

Third version

Wanderer in the black wind; softly dry reeds whisper
In the silence of the moor. Against grey skies
A flight of wild birds follows;
Straight across gloomy waters.

Ferment. In the derelict hut
Foulness flutters up with black wings;
Crippled birches sigh in the wind.

Evening in deserted tavern. The homeward path is shrouded
By gentle melancholy of grazing herds,
Appearance of night: toads surface from silver waters.

IN SPRING

Softly from dark steps snow sank away,
In the shade of the tree
Lovers raise their rosy eyelids.

Dark calls of the boatsmen are ever followed by
Star and night;
And their oars softly beat time.

Soon by the derelict wall will bloom
Violets,
The brow of the lonesome will ever so calmly grow green.

EVENING IN LANS

Second version

Rambling through the fading light of summer
Past sheaves of yellowed corn. Under whitened arches,
Where the swallow flew out and in, we drank ardent wine.

Lovely: O melancholy and crimson laughter.
Evening and the dark odours of greenery
Cool our glowing brow with thrills.

Silberne Wasser rinnen über die Stufen des Walds,
Die Nacht und sprachlos ein vergessenes Leben.
Freund; die belaubten Stege ins Dorf.

AM MÖNCHSBERG

Zweite Fassung

Wo im Schatten herbstlicher Ulmen der verfallene Pfad hinabsinkt,
Ferne den Hütten von Laub, schlafenden Hirten,
Immer folgt dem Wandrer die dunkle Gestalt der Kühle

Über knöchernen Steg, die hyazinthene Stimme des Knaben,
Leise sagend die vergessene Legende des Walds,
Sanfter ein Krankes nun die wilde Klage des Bruders.

Also rührt ein spärliches Grün das Knie des Fremdlings,
Das versteinerte Haupt;
Näher rauscht der blaue Quell die Klage der Frauen.

KASPAR HAUSER LIED

Für Bessie Loos

Er wahrlich liebte die Sonne, die purpurn den Hügel hinabstieg,
Die Wege des Walds, den singenden Schwarzvogel
Und die Freude des Grüns.

Ernsthaft war sein Wohnen im Schatten des Baums
Und rein sein Antlitz.
Gott sprach eine sanfte Flamme zu seinem Herzen:
O Mensch!

Stille fand sein Schritt die Stadt am Abend;
Die dunkle Klage seines Munds:
Ich will ein Reiter werden.

Ihm aber folgte Busch und Tier,
Haus und Dämmergarten weißer Menschen

Silver waters run over the tiers of the forest,
Night and speechless a life unrecalled.
Friend; the leafy paths into the village.

BY THE MÖNCHSBERG

Second version

Where in the shade of autumn elms the derelict track sinks down,
Far from the leafy huts, sleeping shepherds,
The dark figure of coolness ever follows the wanderer

Over skeletal paths, the hyacinth voice of the young boy,
Softly telling the forgotten legend of the forest,
Gentler, now ailing, the brother's wild lament.

Just so sparse greenery touches the knee of the stranger,
The head turned to stone;
Closer the blue source murmurs the women's lament.

KASPAR HAUSER SONG

For Bessie Loos

He truly loved the sun which in crimson descended the hillside,
The paths of the forest, the black singing bird
And the joys of greenery.

Gravely he dwelt in the shade of the tree
And pure his countenance.
God spoke a gentle flame to his heart;
O Man!

Softly his tread found the city at eventide;
The dark lament of his mouth:
I want to be a rider.

Yet he was stalked by bush and beast,
House and dusky garden of white people,

Und sein Mörder suchte nach ihm.

Frühling und Sommer und schön der Herbst
Des Gerechten, sein leiser Schritt
An den dunklen Zimmern Träumender hin.
Nachts blieb er mit seinem Stern allein;

Sah, daß Schnee fiel in kahles Gezweig
Und im dämmernden Hausflur den Schatten des Mörders.

Silbern sank des Ungebornen Haupt hin.

NACHTS

Die Bläue meiner Augen ist erloschen in dieser Nacht,
Das rote Gold meines Herzens. O! wie stille brannte das Licht.
Dein blauer Mantel umfing den Sinkenden;
Dein roter Mund besiegelte des Freundes Umnachtung.

VERWANDLUNG DES BÖSEN

Zweite Fassung

Herbst: schwarzes Schreiten am Waldsaum; Minute stummer Zerstörung;
auflauscht die Stirne des Aussätzigen unter dem kahlen Baum. Lang-
vergangener Abend, der nun über die Stufen von Moos sinkt; November.
Eine Glocke läutet und der Hirt führt eine Herde von schwarzen und roten
Pferden ins Dorf. Unter dem Haselgebüsch weidet der grüne Jäger ein Wild
aus. Seine Hände rauchen von Blut und der Schatten des Tiers seufzt im
Laub über den Augen des Mannes, braun und schweigsam; der Wald.
Krähen, die sich zerstreuen; drei. Ihr Flug gleicht einer Sonate, voll
verblichener Akkorde und männlicher Schwermut; leise löst sich eine
goldene Wolke auf. Bei der Mühle zünden Knaben ein Feuer an. Flamme ist
des Bleichsten Bruder und jener lacht vergraben in sein purpurnes Haar;
oder es ist ein Ort des Mordes, an dem ein steiniger Weg vorbeiführt. Die
Berberitzen sind verschwunden, jahrlang träumt es in bleierner Luft unter
den Föhren; Angst, grünes Dunkel, das Gurgeln eines Ertrinkenden: aus
dem Sternenweiher zieht der Fischer einen großen, schwarzen Fisch, Antlitz

And his murderer sought him.

Spring and summer and lovely the autumn
Of the just man, his quiet tread
Past the dark chambers of those who dream.
At night he remained alone with his star;

Saw that snow fell into naked branches
And in the dusky hallway the shade of the murderer.

All silver, the head of the unborn sank low.

AT NIGHT

The blueness of my eyes has gone out this night,
The red gold of my heart. O how tranquil the light shone.
Your blue mantle enfolded the sinking man;
Your red mouth sealed your friend's dark derangement.

TRANSFORMATION OF EVIL

Second version

Autumn: black striding by the forest's edge; minute of silent destruction; the
leper's brow listens furtively beneath the leafless tree. Long-vanished even-
ing now sinking down over the mossy steps; November. A bell tolls and the
shepherd leads a herd of black and red horses into the village. Under the
hazel bushes the green huntsman disembowels some game. His hands are
smoking with blood and the animal's shadow sighs amid foliage above the
man's eyes, brown and mute; the forest. Crows that scatter; three. Their
flight is like a sonata, full of faded chords and manly melancholy; quietly a
golden cloud dissolves. By the mill boys are lighting a fire. Flame is brother to
the palest and he laughs, buried in his crimson hair; or it is a place of murder
past which a stony way leads. The berberis plants have vanished, for years
past a dream persists in leaden air beneath the firs; fear, green darkness, the
gurgle of a drowning man: out of the starry pond the fisherman draws a great
black fish, the countenance full of cruelty and madness. The voices of the
reeds, of quarrelling men behind, that man rocks in a red boat over freezing

voll Grausamkeit und Irrsinn. Die Stimmen des Rohrs, hadernder Männer im Rücken schaukelt jener auf rotem Kahn über frierende Herbstwasser, lebend in dunklen Sagen seines Geschlechts und die Augen steinern über Nächte und jungfräuliche Schrecken aufgetan. Böse.

Was zwingt dich still zu stehen auf der verfallenen Stiege, im Haus deiner Väter? Bleierne Schwärze. Was hebst du mit silberner Hand an die Augen; und die Lider sinken wie trunken von Mohn ? Aber durch die Mauer von Stein siehst du den Sternenhimmel, die Milchstraße, den Saturn; rot. Rasend an die Mauer von Stein klopft der kahle Baum. Du auf verfallenen Stufen: Baum, Stern, Stein ! Du, ein blaues Tier, das leise zittert; du, der bleiche Priester, der es hinschlachtet am schwarzen Altar. O dein Lächeln im Dunkel, traurig und böse, daß ein Kind im Schlaf erbleicht. Eine rote Flamme sprang aus deiner Hand und ein Nachtfalter verbrannte daran. O die Flöte des Lichts; o die Flöte des Tods. Was zwang dich still zu stehen auf verfallener Stiege, im Haus deiner Väter? Drunten ans Tor klopft ein Engel mit kristallnem Finger.

O die Hölle des Schlafs; dunkle Gasse, braunes Gärtchen. Leise läutet im blauen Abend der Toten Gestalt. Grüne Blümchen umgaukeln sie und ihr Antlitz hat sie verlassen. Oder es neigt sich verblichen über die kalte Stirne des Mörders im Dunkel des Hausflurs; Anbetung, purpurne Flamme der Wollust; hinsterbend stürzte über schwarze Stufen der Schläfer ins Dunkel.

Jemand verließ dich am Kreuzweg und du schaust lange zurück. Silberner Schritt im Schatten verkrüppelter Apfelbäumchen. Purpurn leuchtet die Frucht im schwarzen Geäst und im Gras häutet sich die Schlange. O! das Dunkel; der Schweiß, der auf die eisige Stirne tritt und die traurigen Träume im Wein, in der Dorfschenke unter schwarzverrauchtem Gebälk. Du, noch Wildnis, die rosige Inseln zaubert aus dem braunen Tabaksgewölk und aus dem Innern den wilden Schrei eines Greifen holt, wenn er um schwarze Klippen jagt in Meer, Sturm und Eis. Du, ein grünes Metall und innen ein feuriges Gesicht, das hingehen will und singen vom Beinerhügel finstere Zeiten und den flammenden Sturz des Engels. O Verzweiflung, die mit stummem Schrei ins Knie bricht.

Ein Toter besucht dich. Aus dem Herzen rinnt das selbstvergossene Blut und in schwarzer Braue nistet unsäglicher Augenblick; dunkle Begegnung. Du – ein purpurner Mond, da jener im grünen Schatten des Ölbaums erscheint. Dem folgt unvergängliche Nacht.

autumn waters, living in dark legends of his race, his eyes opened stonily upon nights and virginal terrors. Evil.

What compels you to stand still on the derelict stairs in the house of your ancestors? Leaden blackness. What is it you raise to your eyes with silver hand; and the eyelids droop as if drunk with opium? But through the wall of stone you see the starry sky, the Milky Way, Saturn; red. Crazed, the barren tree knocks upon the wall of stone. You on derelict steps: tree, star, stone! You, a blue animal that silently trembles; you, the pale priest who sacrifices it upon the black altar. O your smile in the dark, sad and evil, such that a child blanches in its sleep. A red flame sprang from your hand and a night moth was burnt in it. O flute of light; o flute of death. What compelled you to stand still on the derelict stairs in the house of your ancestors? Below an angel is knocking at the gate with crystal finger.

O the hell of sleep; dark alley, little brown garden. In the evening quietly tolls the form of the dead. Little green flowers sport about them and their countenance has left them. Or it bends pale over the cold forehead of the murderer in the dark of the hallway; adulation, crimson flame of volupt-uousness; in the throes of death the sleeper plunged over black steps into darkness.

Someone deserted you at the crossroads and you glance back for a long time. Silver strides in the shade of crippled little apple trees. Crimson gleams the fruit among the black branches and in the grass the snake sheds its skin. O! the darkness; the sweat that forms on the icy brow and the sad dreams in wine, in the village tavern beneath smoke-blackened beams. You, still a wilderness, which conjures rosy islands from brown tobacco clouds and calls forth from within the savage cry of a gryphon, as he chases about black cliffs in sea, storm and ice. You, a green metal and within a fiery face that will go out and sing of dark times from the hill of bones and the flaming fall of the angel. O! despair that falls to its knees with dumb cry.

A dead man visits you. Out of the heart runs the self-spilt blood and in black eyebrows nests the ineffable moment; dark encounter. You – a crimson moon, as the One appears in the green shade of the olive tree. Thereafter follows eternal night.

IM PARK

Wieder wandelnd im alten Park,
O! Stille gelb und roter Blumen.
Ihr auch trauert, ihr sanften Götter,
Und das herbstliche Gold der Ulme.
Reglos ragt am bläulichen Weiher
Das Rohr, verstummt am Abend die Drossel.
O! dann neige auch du die Stirne
Vor der Ahnen verfallenem Marmor.

EIN WINTERABEND

Zweite Fassung

Wenn der Schnee ans Fenster fällt,
Lang die Abendglocke läutet,
Vielen ist der Tisch bereitet
Und das Haus ist wohlbestellt.

Mancher auf der Wanderschaft
Kommt ans Tor auf dunklen Pfaden.
Golden blüht der Baum der Gnaden
Aus der Erde kühlem Saft.

Wanderer tritt still herein;
Schmerz versteinerte die Schwelle.
Da erglänzt in reiner Helle
Auf dem Tische Brot und Wein.

IN THE PARK

Wandering once more in the ancient park,
O! Silence of the red and yellow flower.
You also mourn, you gentle gods,
And the autumn gold of the elm.
Rigid there rise by the pale blue pond
Reeds, the thrush's evening song ceases.
O! Then you also stoop low
Before your forefathers' marble decay.

A WINTER'S EVE

Second version

When snow falls against the window,
Long the evening bell keeps tolling,
Many find their table ready
And the house is well supplied.

Many a wanderer on his journey
Comes by dark paths to the doorway.
Golden flowers the tree of bounty
Out of the cool sap of earth.

Wanderer steps silent indoors;
Pain has petrified the threshold.
Then shines out in purest radiance
On the table bread and wine.

1

Es dämmert. Zum Brunnen gehn die alten Fraun.
Im Dunkel der Kastanien lacht ein Rot.
Aus einem Laden rinnt ein Duft von Brot
Und Sonnenblumen sinken übern Zaun.

Am Fluß die Schenke tönt noch lau und leis.
Guitarre summt; ein Klimperklang von Geld.
Ein Heiligenschein auf jene Kleine fällt,
Die vor der Glastür wartet sanft und weiß.

O! blauer Glanz, den sie in Scheiben weckt,
Umrahmt von Dornen, schwarz und starrverzückt.
Ein krummer Schreiber lächelt wie verrückt
Ins Wasser, das ein wilder Aufruhr schreckt.

2

Am Abend säumt die Pest ihr blau Gewand
Und leise schließt die Tür ein finstrer Gast.
Durchs Fenster sinkt des Ahorns schwarze Last;
Ein Knabe legt die Stirn in ihre Hand.

Oft sinken ihre Lider bös und schwer.
Des Kindes Hände rinnen durch ihr Haar
Und seine Tränen stürzen heiß und klar
In ihre Augenhöhlen schwarz und leer.

Ein Nest von scharlachfarbnen Schlangen bäumt
Sich träg in ihrem aufgewühlten Schoß.
Die Arme lassen ein Erstorbenes los,
Das eines Teppichs Traurigkeit umsäumt.

3

Ins braune Gärtchen tönt ein Glockenspiel.
Im Dunkel der Kastanien schwebt ein Blau,
Der süße Mantel einer fremden Frau.
Resedenduft; und glühendes Gefühl

1

Twilight comes. The aged women go to the well.
In the dark shade of the chestnuts redness laughs.
Out of a shop oozes a smell of bread
And sunflowers droop over a fence.

The river inn still echoes soft and quiet.
A guitar hums; a jingling of coin.
A halo is cast upon that little girl,
Who meek and white before the glass door waits.

O! gleam of blue which she calls forth in panes,
Framed by thorns, black and in rapture fixed.
A crooked clerk as though in madness smiles
Into the water which wild tumult stirs.

2

At evening the plague trims her mantle blue
And quietly a sombre guest shuts the door.
The maple's black burden through the window droops;
A young boy lays his forehead in her hand.

Often her eyelids droop wicked and heavy.
The child's hands course through her hair
And his tears burst forth hot and clear
Into her sockets black and void.

A nest of scarlet serpents writhes
In lethargy within her harrowed womb,
Her arms release a thing that's died,
Which borders a carpet's sadness.

3

A carillon carries into the small brown garden,
A blueness hovers in the gloom of chestnut trees.
The gentle cloak of an unknown woman.
Smell of resedas; and a glowing sense

Des Bösen. Die feuchte Stirn beugt kalt und bleich
Sich über Unrat, drin die Ratte wühlt,
Vom Scharlachglanz der Sterne lau umspült;
Im Garten fallen Äpfel dumpf und weich.

Die Nacht ist schwarz. Gespenstisch bläht der Föhn
Des wandelnden Knaben weißes Schlafgewand
Und leise greift in seinen Mund die Hand
Der Toten. Sonja lächelt sanft und schön.

SONJA

Abend kehrt in alten Garten;
Sonjas Leben, blaue Stille.
Wilder Vögel Wanderfahrten;
Kahler Baum in Herbst und Stille.

Sonnenblume, sanftgeneigte
Über Sonjas weißes Leben.
Wunde, rote, niegezeigte
Läßt in dunklen Zimmern leben,

Wo die blauen Glocken läuten;
Sonjas Schritt und sanfte Stille.
Sterbend Tier grüßt im Entgleiten,
Kahler Baum in Herbst und Stille.

Sonne alter Tage leuchtet
Über Sonjas weiße Brauen,
Schnee, der ihre Wangen feuchtet,
Und die Wildnis ihrer Brauen.

ENTLANG

Geschnitten sind Korn und Traube,
Der Weiler in Herbst und Ruh.
Hammer und Amboß klingt immerzu,
Lachen in purpurner Laube.

Of evil. The moist brow stoops cold and pale
Over some refuse which rats plunder,
Washed mildly round by scarlet gleam of stars;
The apples in the garden fall soft and with a thud.

The night is black. Ghostly the southern breeze billows
The wandering boy's white night clothes
And in stealth the dead woman's hand gropes
His mouth. Sonja's smile is mild and lovely.

SONJA

Evening comes to ancient garden;
Sonja's life, a deep blue stillness.
Wild birds bound on distant wanderings;
Naked tree in autumn silence.

Sunflower, bowed in gentle gesture
Over Sonja's life of whiteness.
Blood-red wound, revealed to no one
Limits life to darkened chambers,

Where blue bells are ever tolling;
Sonja's tread and gentle silence.
Dying beast greets in expiring,
Naked tree in autumn silence.

Sun of bygone days is gleaming
Over Sonja's brows of whiteness,
Snowfall that her cheek has moistened,
And the wild waste of her eyebrows.

ALONG

Corn and grapevine have been cut,
The hamlet in autumn and repose.
Hammer and anvil ring ever on,
Laughter in crimson arbor.

Astern von dunklen Zäunen
Bring dem weißen Kind.
Sag wie lang wir gestorben sind;
Sonne will schwarz erscheinen.

Rotes Fischlein im Weiher;
Stirn, die sich fürchtig belauscht;
Abendwind leise ans Fenster rauscht,
Blaues Orgelgeleier.

Stern und heimlich Gefunkel
Läßt noch einmal aufschaun.
Erscheinung der Mutter in Schmerz und Graun;
Schwarze Reseden im Dunkel.

HERBSTSEELE

Zweite Fassung

Jägerruf und Blutgebell;
Hinter Kreuz und braunem Hügel
Blindet sacht der Weiherspiegel,
Schreit der Habicht hart und hell.

Über Stoppelfeld und Pfad
Banget schon ein schwarzes Schweigen;
Reiner Himmel in den Zweigen;
Nur der Bach rinnt still und stad.

Bald entgleitet Fisch und Wild.
Blaue Seele, dunkles Wandern
Schied uns bald von Lieben, Andern.
Abend wechselt Sinn und Bild.

Rechten Lebens Brot und Wein,
Gott in deine milden Hände
Legt der Mensch das dunkle Ende,
Alle Schuld und rote Pein.

Fetch the asters from dark fences
For the small white child.
Say how long we took in dying;
Sun's about to rise in black.

Little red fish in the pond;
Fearful the brow's self-perusal;
Evening breeze blows softly at the window,
Blue organ droning.

Star and secret sparkle
Bids you raise your eyes once more.
Mother appearing in pain and horror;
Black resedas in the gloom.

AUTUMN SOUL

Second version

Hunting calls and blood-baying;
Beyond cross and brown hill
The pond's mirror gently blinds one,
The hawk's screech is hard and clear.

Over stubble-field and path
A black silence lurks in fear;
Purest sky amid the branches;
Only the brook runs silent and still.

Fish and game soon slip away.
Blue soul, darksome wandering
Soon severed us from loved ones, others.
Evening alters sense and image.

Bread and wine of sinless living,
God into your mild hands
Man places the dark ending,
All guilt and red torment.

AFRA

Zweite Fassung

Ein Kind mit braunem Haar. Gebet und Amen
Verdunkeln still die abendliche Kühle
Und Afras Lächeln rot in gelbem Rahmen
Von Sonnenblumen, Angst und grauer Schwüle.

Gehüllt in blauen Mantel sah vor Zeiten
Der Mönch sie fromm gemalt an Kirchenfenstern;
Das will in Schmerzen freundlich noch geleiten,
Wenn ihre Sterne durch sein Blut gespenstern.

Herbstuntergang; und des Hollunders Schweigen.
Die Stirne rührt des Wassers blaue Regung,
Ein härnes Tuch gelegt auf eine Bahre.

Verfaulte Früchte fallen von den Zweigen;
Unsäglich ist der Vögel Flug, Begegnung
Mit Sterbenden; dem folgen dunkle Jahre.

DER HERBST DES EINSAMEN

Der dunkle Herbst kehrt ein voll Frucht und Fülle,
Vergilbter Glanz von schönen Sommertagen.
Ein reines Blau tritt aus verfallener Hülle;
Der Flug der Vögel tönt von alten Sagen.
Gekeltert ist der Wein, die milde Stille
Erfüllt von leiser Antwort dunkler Fragen.

Und hier und dort ein Kreuz auf ödem Hügel;
Im roten Wald verliert sich eine Herde.
Die Wolke wandert übern Weiherspiegel;
Es ruht des Landmanns ruhige Geberde.
Sehr leise rührt des Abends blauer Flügel
Ein Dach von dürrem Stroh, die schwarze Erde.

Bald nisten Sterne in des Müden Brauen;
In kühle Stuben kehrt ein still Bescheiden
Und Engel treten leise aus den blauen
Augen der Liebenden, die sanfter leiden.
Es rauscht das Rohr; anfällt ein knöchern Grauen,
Wenn schwarz der Tau tropft von den kahlen Weiden.

AFRA

Second version

A child with brown hair. Prayer and Amen
Silently darken the evening coolness
And Afra's smile red in the yellow frame
Of sunflowers, fear and grey sultriness.

Wrapped in blue cloak the monk saw her
Ages past, piously painted on church windows;
This still through pain can be a friendly guide,
Whenever her stars are haunting in his blood.

Autumn's decline; and silence of the elder bush.
The brow touches the water's blue motion,
A cloth of hair placed on a bier.

Rotted fruit falls from the branches;
Ineffable is the flight of birds, encounter
With the dying; thereafter follow dark years.

THE AUTUMN OF THE LONELY

Dark autumn comes all filled with fruit and plenty,
The yellowed gleam of lovely summer days.
Pure blueness breaks from a decayed shell;
The flight of birds resounds with ancient legends.
The wine is pressed, the mild silence
Replete with obscure questions of a gentle reply.

And here and there a cross upon a desolate hill;
A herd is lost to sight in the red wood.
The cloud drifts over the mirror of the pond;
The peasant's peaceful gesture is at rest.
Evening's blue wing most gently brushes
A roof of sparse straw, the black earth.

Soon stars will nestle in the tired man's brow;
Into cool chambers steals a calm content
And angels gently enter the blue eyes
Of lovers whose suffering is milder.
Reeds rustle; out springs a bony horror,
When black the dew drips out of barren willows.

RUH UND SCHWEIGEN

Hirten begruben die Sonne im kahlen Wald.
Ein Fischer zog
In härenem Netz den Mond aus frierendem Weiher.

In blauem Kristall
Wohnt der bleiche Mensch, die Wang' an seine Sterne gelehnt;
Oder er neigt das Haupt in purpurnem Schlaf.

Doch immer rührt der schwarze Flug der Vögel
Den Schauenden, das Heilige blauer Blumen,
Denkt die nahe Stille Vergessenes, erloschene Engel.

Wieder nachtet die Stirne in mondenem Gestein;
Ein strahlender Jüngling
Erscheint die Schwester in Herbst und schwarzer Verwesung.

ANIF

Erinnerung: Möven, gleitend über den dunklen Himmel
Männlicher Schwermut.
Stille wohnst du im Schatten der herbstlichen Esche,
Versunken in des Hügels gerechtes Maß;

Immer gehst du den grünen Fluß hinab,
Wenn es Abend geworden,
Tönende Liebe; friedlich begegnet das dunkle Wild,

Ein rosiger Mensch. Trunken von bläulicher Witterung
Rührt die Stirne das sterbende Laub
Und denkt das ernste Antlitz der Mutter;
O, wie alles ins Dunkel hinsinkt;

PEACE AND SILENCE

Shepherds buried the sun in the naked forest.
A fisherman drew
The moon in a net of hair from the freezing pond.

In blue crystal
Dwells the pale man, his cheek leant against his stars;
Or he inclines his head in purple slumber.

Yet the black flight of birds ever touches
The one who gazes, the sacredness of blue flowers,
The nearby silence ponders what is forgotten, extinguished angels.

Once more the brow grows dark in moon-born rocks,
A radiant youth,
Sister appears in autumn and black decay.

ANIF

Remembrance: gulls gliding above the dark heavens
Of manly melancholy.
Tranquil you dwell in the shade of the autumn ash,
Lost in the righteous measure of the hill;

For ever you walk down the green river,
When the evening has come,
Singing Love; the dark prey is encountered in peace,

A rosy person. Drunken with bluish weather
The dying leaves touch the forehead
And think on my mother's grave countenance;
O, how all things sink into darkness;

Die gestrengen Zimmer und das alte Gerät
Der Väter.
Dieses erschüttert die Brust des Fremdlings.
O, ihr Zeichen und Sterne.

Groß ist die Schuld des Geborenen. Weh, ihr goldenen Schauer
Des Todes,
Da die Seele kühlere Blüten träumt.

Immer schreit im kahlen Gezweig der nächtliche Vogel
Über des Mondenen Schritt,
Tönt ein eisiger Wind an den Mauern des Dorfs.

GEBURT

Gebirge: Schwärze, Schweigen und Schnee.
Rot vom Wald niedersteigt die Jagd;
O, die moosigen Blicke des Wilds.

Stille der Mutter; unter schwarzen Tannen
Öffnen sich die schlafenden Hände,
Wenn verfallen der kalte Mond erscheint.

O, die Geburt des Menschen. Nächtlich rauscht
Blaues Wasser im Felsengrund;
Seufzend erblickt sein Bild der gefallene Engel,

Erwacht ein Bleiches in dumpfer Stube.
Zwei Monde
Erglänzen die Augen der steinernen Greisin.

Weh, der Gebärenden Schrei. Mit schwarzem Flügel
Rührt die Knabenschläfe die Nacht,
Schnee, der leise aus purpurner Wolke sinkt.

The stern rooms and the ancient goods
Of forefathers.
This shatters the stranger's breast.
O, you signs and stars.

Great is the guilt of the one who is born. Woe, you golden thrills
Of death,
When the soul dreams cooler blossoms.

Evermore the night bird calls out in the bare branches
Above the moon-child's tread,
An icy wind resounds by the village walls.

BIRTH

Mountains: blackness, silence and snow.
Red from the forest the hunt descends;
O, the mossy glances of the game.

Silence of the mother; beneath black fir trees
The sleeping hands unfold,
When decayed the cold moon appears.

O, the birth of Man. Nightly blue water
Gushes in the valley of rocks;
Sighing the fallen angel glimpses his image,

A pale thing awakens in a musty room.
Two moons
The eyes of the stony old woman start to gleam.

Woe, the scream of those in labour. With black wing
Night brushes the young boy's brow,
Snow that gently sinks down from a crimson cloud.

UNTERGANG

Fünfte Fassung

An Karl Borromaeus Heinrich

Über den weißen Weiher
Sind die wilden Vögel fortgezogen.
Am Abend weht von unseren Sternen ein eisiger Wind.

Über unsere Gräber
Beugt sich die zerbrochene Stirne der Nacht.
Unter Eichen schaukeln wir auf einem silbernen Kahn.

Immer klingen die weißen Mauern der Stadt.
Unter Dornenbogen
O mein Bruder klimmen wir blinde Zeiger gen Mitternacht.

AN EINEN FRÜHVERSTORBENEN

O, der schwarze Engel, der leise aus dem Innern des Baums trat,
Da wir sanfte Gespielen am Abend waren,
Am Rand des bläulichen Brunnens.
Ruhig war unser Schritt, die runden Augen in der braunen Kühle des Herbstes,
O, die purpurne Süße der Sterne.

Jener aber ging die steinernen Stufen des Mönchsbergs hinab,
Ein blaues Lächeln im Antlitz und seltsam verpuppt
In seine stillere Kindheit und starb;
Und im Garten blieb das silberne Antlitz des Freundes zurück,
Lauschend im Laub oder im alten Gestein.

Seele sang den Tod, die grüne Verwesung des Fleisches
Und es war das Rauschen des Walds,
Die inbrünstige Klage des Wildes.
Immer klangen von dämmernden Türmen die blauen Glocken des Abends.

Stunde kam, da jener die Schatten in purpurner Sonne sah,
Die Schatten der Fäulnis in kahlem Geäst;
Abend, da an dämmernder Mauer die Amsel sang,
Der Geist des Frühverstorbenen stille im Zimmer erschien.

DECLINE

Fifth version

To Karl Borromaeus Heinrich

Over the white pond
The wild birds have departed.
At evening an icy wind blows from our stars.

Over our graves
The broken brow of night bends low.
Beneath oaks we sway in a silver boat.

The white walls of the city ever ring.
Beneath arches of thorns
O my brother, we blind clock-hands climb towards midnight.

TO ONE WHO DIED YOUNG

O, the black angel who quietly stepped from the core of the tree,
When at eventide we gently played in youth
By the rim of the bluish well
Calm was our step, round eyes in the brown coolness of autumn,
O, the crimson sweetness of the stars.

Yet he descended the stony steps of the Monk's Hill,
A blue smile on his features and strangely cocooned
In his quieter childhood, and died;
And the friend's silver countenance remained in the garden,
Listening in the leaves or amongst the ancient stones.

Soul sang death, the green decay of the flesh
And it was the rustling sound of the forest,
The fervent lament of the prey.
The blue evening bells ever pealed from twilit towers.

The hour came when he saw the shades in the crimson sun,
The shades of decay in naked boughs;
Evening, when the blackbird sang by the twilit wall,
The ghost of the one who died young silently appeared in the room.

O, das Blut, das aus der Kehle des Tönenden rinnt,
Blaue Blume; o die feurige Träne
Geweint in die Nacht.

Goldene Wolke und Zeit. In einsamer Kammer
Lädst du öfter den Toten zu Gast,
Wandelst in trautem Gespräch unter Ulmen den grünen Fluß hinab.

GEISTLICHE DÄMMERUNG

Zweite Fassung

Stille begegnet am Saum des Waldes
Ein dunkles Wild;
Am Hügel endet leise der Abendwind,

Verstummt die Klage der Amsel,
Und die sanften Flöten des Herbstes
Schweigen im Rohr.

Auf schwarzer Wolke
Befährst du trunken von Mohn
Den nächtigen Weiher,

Den Sternenhimmel.
Immer tönt der Schwester mondene Stimme
Durch die geistliche Nacht.

ABENDLÄNDISCHES LIED

O der Seele nächtlicher Flügelschlag:
Hirten gingen wir einst an dämmernden Wäldern hin
Und es folgte das rote Wild, die grüne Blume und der lallende Quell
Demutsvoll. O, der uralte Ton des Heimchens,
Blut blühend am Opferstein
Und der Schrei des einsamen Vogels über der grünen Stille des Teichs.

O, ihr Kreuzzüge und glühenden Martern
Des Fleisches, Fallen purpurner Früchte

O, blood that runs from the throat of the singing voice,
Blue flower; o fiery tear
Wept into the night.

Golden cloud and time. In a lonely chamber
You often bid the dead man be your guest,
Down the green river you wander in intimate talk under elms.

SPIRITUAL TWILIGHT

Second version

Silent by the forest's edge dark game
Is encountered;
By the hill the evening breeze gently dies,

The blackbird's lament falls silent,
And the soft flutes of autumn
Are at peace in the reeds.

Upon a black cloud
You travel drunk with poppyseed
The night-dark pond,

The starry heavens.
Sister's moon-like voice ever sounds
Through the sacred night.

SONG OF THE WESTERN WORLD

O the soul's nocturnal wingbeat;
Shepherds, we once walked by twilit forests
And there followed red game, the green flower and the babbling spring
In humility. O, the age-old sound of the cricket,
Blood blossoming by the altar-stone
And the cry of the solitary bird above the green silence of the pool.

O, you crusades and glowing torments
Of the flesh, the fall of crimson fruit

Im Abendgarten, wo vor Zeiten die frommen Jünger gegangen,
Kriegsleute nun, erwachend aus Wunden und Sternenträumen.
O, das sanfte Zyanenbündel der Nacht.

O, ihr Zeiten der Stille und goldener Herbste,
Da wir friedliche Mönche die purpurne Traube gekeltert;
Und rings erglänzten Hügel und Wald.
O, ihr Jagden und Schlösser; Ruh des Abends,
Da in seiner Kammer der Mensch Gerechtes sann,
In stummem Gebet um Gottes lebendiges Haupt rang.

O, die bittere Stunde des Untergangs,
Da wir ein steinernes Antlitz in schwarzen Wassern beschaun.
Aber strahlend heben die silbernen Lider die Liebenden:
E i n Geschlecht. Weihrauch strömt von rosigen Kissen
Und der süße Gesang der Auferstandenen.

VERKLÄRUNG

Wenn es Abend wird,
Verläßt dich leise ein blaues Antlitz.
Ein kleiner Vogel singt im Tamarindenbaum.

Ein sanfter Mönch
Faltet die erstorbenen Hände.
Ein weißer Engel sucht Marien heim.

Ein nächtiger Kranz
Von Veilchen, Korn und purpurnen Trauben
Ist das Jahr des Schauenden.

Zu deinen Füßen
Öffnen sich die Gräber der Toten,
Wenn du die Stirne in die silbernen Hände legst.

Stille wohnt
An deinem Mund der herbstliche Mond,
Trunken von Mohnsaft dunkler Gesang;

Blaue Blume,
Die leise tönt in vergilbtem Gestein.

In the evening garden, where ages past pious disciples walked,
Warriers now, waking from wounds and star-dreams.
O, the gentle cornflower-spray of night.

O, you times of silence and golden autumns,
When we peaceful monks trod the crimson grape,
And all around hill and forest began to glow.
O, you hunts and castles; rest at eventide,
When in his chamber Man pondered what is just,
In silent prayer wrestled for God's living head.

O, the bitter hour of decline,
When we gaze upon a stony countenance in black waters.
Yet lovers radiant raise their silver eyelids:
One sex. Incense streams from rosy pillows
And the sweet song of the resurrected.

TRANSFIGURATION

When evening comes,
A blue countenance gently leaves you.
A little bird sings in the tamarind-tree.

A gentle monk
Folds his deceased hands.
A white angel visits Mary.

A nocturnal wreath
Of violets, corn and crimson grapes
Is the year of the gazer.

At your feet
The graves of the dead open,
When you rest your brow in your silver hands.

Silent dwells
By your mouth the autumn moon,
Dark singing drunk with poppy juice;

Blue flower
Which quietly rings in the yellowing rocks.

FÖHN

Blinde Klage im Wind, mondene Wintertage,
Kindheit, leise verhallen die Schritte an schwarzer Hecke,
Langes Abendgeläut.
Leise kommt die weiße Nacht gezogen,

Verwandelt in purpurne Träume Schmerz und Plage
Des steinigen Lebens,
Daß nimmer der dornige Stachel ablasse vom verwesenden Leib.

Tief im Schlummer aufseufzt die bange Seele,

Tief der Wind in zerbrochenen Bäumen,
Und es schwankt die Klagegestalt
Der Mutter durch den einsamen Wald

Dieser schweigenden Trauer; Nächte,
Erfüllt von Tränen, feurigen Engeln.
Silbern zerschellt an kahler Mauer ein kindlich Gerippe.

DER WANDERER
Zweite Fassung

Immer lehnt am Hügel die weiße Nacht,
Wo in Silbertönen die Pappel ragt,
Stern' und Steine sind.

Schlafend wölbt sich über den Gießbach der Steg,
Folgt dem Knaben ein erstorbenes Antlitz,
Sichelmond in rosiger Schlucht

Ferne preisenden Hirten. In altem Gestein
Schaut aus kristallenen Augen die Kröte,
Erwacht der blühende Wind, die Vogelstimme des Totengleichen
Und die Schritte ergrünen leise im Wald.

Dieses erinnert an Baum und Tier. Langsame Stufen von Moos;
Und der Mond,
Der glänzend in traurigen Wassern versinkt.

Jener kehrt wieder und wandelt an grünem Gestade,
Schaukelt auf schwarzem Gondelschiffchen durch die verfallene Stadt.

FÖHN

Blind lament in the wind, moon-like winter days,
Childhood, the footsteps quietly die away by the black hedge,
Long tolling of evening bells.
The white night quietly draws on,

Transforms pain and plague into crimson dreams
Of stony life,
That the thorny sting never ceases to vex the decaying body.

Deep in sleep the fearful soul draws a sigh,

Deep the wind in broken trees,
And the sorrowing figure
Of mother sways through the lonely forest

Of this mute mourning; nights,
Filled with tears, fiery angels.
All silver a childlike skeleton shatters upon a bare wall.

THE WANDERER

Second version

The white night ever leans against the hill,
Where in silver tones the poplar towers,
Stars and stones are.

Asleep the little bridge arches over the torrent,
A deceased countenance pursues the young boy,
Moon-sickle in roseate gorge

Far from lauding shepherds. Amid ancient rocks
The toad peers with crystalline eyes,
The blossoming breeze awakens, the bird-voice of the deathlike
And one's steps gently grow green in the forest.

This recalls tree and beast. Slow steps of moss;
And the moon
Which sinks gleaming into sad waters.

He returns again and roams along green banks,
Rocks in a little black gondola through the derelict town.

KARL KRAUS

Weißer Hohepriester der Wahrheit,
Kristallne Stimme, in der Gottes eisiger Odem wohnt,
Zürnender Magier,
Dem unter flammendem Mantel der blaue Panzer des Kriegers klirrt.

AN DIE VERSTUMMTEN

O, der Wahnsinn der großen Stadt, da am Abend
An schwarzer Mauer verkrüppelte Bäume starren,
Aus silberner Maske der Geist des Bösen schaut;
Licht mit magnetischer Geißel die steinerne Nacht verdrängt.
O, das versunkene Läuten der Abendglocken.

Hure, die in eisigen Schauern ein totes Kindlein gebart.
Rasend peitscht Gottes Zorn die Stirne des Besessenen,
Purpurne Seuche, Hunger, der grüne Augen zerbricht.
O, das gräßliche Lachen des Golds.

Aber stille blutet in dunkler Höhle stummere Menschheit,
Fügt aus harten Metallen das erlösende Haupt.

PASSION
Dritte Fassung

Wenn Orpheus silbern die Laute rührt,
Beklagend ein Totes im Abendgarten,
Wer bist du Ruhendes unter hohen Bäumen?
Es rauscht die Klage das herbstliche Rohr,
Der blaue Teich,
Hinsterbend unter grünenden Bäumen
Und folgend dem Schatten der Schwester;
Dunkle Liebe
Eines wilden Geschlechts,
Dem auf goldenen Rädern der Tag davonrauscht.
Stille Nacht.

KARL KRAUS

White high priest of truth,
Crystal voice wherein God's icy breath dwells.
Wrathful magus,
Whose blue warrior's breastplate beneath blazing mantle rings.

TO THOSE GROWN SILENT

O, the madness of the great city, when at evening
Crippled trees stand rigid by the black wall.
The spirit of evil stares from a silver mask;
Light disperses stony night with magnetic scourge.
O, the sunken ringing of evening bells.

Whore, who with icy shudders gives birth to a dead child.
Raging, God's wrath lashes the brow of the one possessed,
Scarlet contagion, hunger that shatters green eyes.
O, the horrible laughter of gold.

But in the dark cave a muter humanity bleeds,
Fashions from hard metals the redeeming head.

PASSION

Third version

When Orpheus with silver touch rouses the lyre,
Lamenting a dead thing in the evening garden,
Who are you at rest under tall trees?
Autumn leaves rustle their lament,
The blue pond,
Expiring beneath fresh green trees
And following sister's shadow;
Dark love
Of a savage race,
Whose day rushes to its close on golden wheels.
Silent night.

Unter finsteren Tannen
Mischten zwei Wölfe ihr Blut
In steinerner Umarmung; ein Goldnes
Verlor sich die Wolke über dem Steg,
Geduld und Schweigen der Kindheit.
Wieder begegnet der zarte Leichnam
Am Tritonsteich
Schlummernd in seinem hyazinthenen Haar.
Daß endlich zerbräche das kühle Haupt!

Denn immer folgt, ein blaues Wild,
Ein Äugendes unter dämmernden Bäumen,
Dieser dunkleren Pfaden
Wachend und bewegt von nächtigem Wohllaut,
Sanftem Wahnsinn;
Oder es tönte dunkler Verzückung
Voll das Saitenspiel
Zu den kühlen Füßen der Büßerin
In der steinernen Stadt.

SIEBENGESANG DES TODES

Bläulich dämmert der Frühling, unter saugenden Bäumen
Wandert ein Dunkles in Abend und Untergang,
Lauschend der sanften Klage der Amsel.
Schweigend erscheint die Nacht, ein blutendes Wild,
Das langsam hinsinkt am Hügel.

In feuchter Luft schwankt blühendes Apfelgezweig,
Löst silbern sich Verschlungenes,
Hinsterbend aus nächtigen Augen; fallende Sterne;
Sanfter Gesang der Kindheit.

Erscheinender stieg der Schläfer den schwarzen Wald hinab,
Und es rauschte ein blauer Quell im Grund,
Daß jener leise die bleichen Lider aufhob
Über sein schneeiges Antlitz;

Under sombre firs
Two wolves mingled their blood
In stony embrace; a thing of gold
The cloud vanished above the path,
Patience and silence of childhood.
Once more the tender corpse is encountered
By the Triton pond
Slumbering in its hyacinth hair.
If only the chill head would shatter at last!

For there ever follows, a blue prey,
A thing seeking under twilit trees
Along these darker paths
Alert and moved by nightly melody,
Gentle madness;
Or there sounded the music of strings
Filled with dark ecstasy
At the cool feet of the penitent
In the stony city.

SEVENFOLD SONG OF DEATH

Spring fades in bluish twilight; under sucking trees
A dark thing wanders in evening and decline,
Listening to the blackbird's gentle lament.
Silently night appears, a wild thing bleeding
Which slowly sinks to earth on the hillside.

Blossoming apple boughs sway in the moist air,
What is entangled finds silvery release,
Dying away in night-dark eyes; falling stars;
Gentle song of childhood.

Further appearing the sleeper descended along the black forest
And a blue spring murmured in the valley,
That he quietly raised his blue eyelids
Over his snowy countenance;

Und es jagte der Mond ein rotes Tier
Aus seiner Höhle;
Und es starb in Seufzern die dunkle Klage der Frauen.

Strahlender hob die Hände zu seinem Stern
Der weiße Fremdling;
Schweigend verläßt ein Totes das verfallene Haus.

O des Menschen verweste Gestalt: gefügt aus kalten Metallen,
Nacht und Schrecken versunkener Wälder
Und der sengenden Wildnis des Tiers;
Windesstille der Seele.

Auf schwärzlichem Kahn fuhr jener schimmernde Ströme hinab,
Purpurner Sterne voll, und es sank
Friedlich das ergrünte Gezweig auf ihn,
Mohn aus silberner Wolke.

WINTERNACHT

Es ist Schnee gefallen. Nach Mitternacht verläßt du betrunken von purpur-
nem Wein den dunklen Bezirk der Menschen, die rote Flamme ihres
Herdes. O die Finsternis!

Schwarzer Frost. Die Erde ist hart, nach Bitterem schmeckt die Luft.
Deine Sterne schließen sich zu bösen Zeichen.

Mit versteinerten Schritten stampfst du am Bahndamm hin, mit runden
Augen, wie ein Soldat, der eine schwarze Schanze stürmt. Avanti!

Bitterer Schnee und Mond!

Ein roter Wolf, den ein Engel würgt. Deine Beine klirren schreitend wie
blaues Eis und ein Lächeln voll Trauer und Hochmut hat dein Antlitz
versteinert und die Stirne erbleicht vor der Wollust des Frostes;

oder sie neigt sich schweigend über den Schlaf eines Wächters, der in
seiner hölzernen Hütte hinsank.

Frost und Rauch. Ein weißes Sternenhemd verbrennt die tragenden
Schultern und Gottes Geier zerfleischen dein metallenes Herz.

O der steinerne Hügel. Stille schmilzt und vergessen der kühle Leib im
silbernen Schnee hin.

Schwarz ist der Schlaf. Das Ohr folgt lange den Pfaden der Sterne im Eis.

Beim Erwachen klangen die Glocken im Dorf. Aus dem östlichen Tor trat
silbern der rosige Tag.

And the moon chased a red animal
From its cave;
And the dark lament of the women died in sighs.

Yet more radiant the white stranger
Raised his hands up to his star;
Silent a dead thing leaves the derelict house.

O the decayed figure of Man: composed of cold metals,
Night and terrors of sunken forests
And the searing wilderness of the beast;
Deep calm of the soul.

On blackish barge he floated down glinting streams,
Filled with scarlet stars, and tranquil
The fresh green branches sank down over him,
Poppyseed from a silver cloud.

WINTER NIGHT

Snow has fallen. After midnight, drunk with purple wine you leave the dark abode of humans, the red flame of their hearth. O the darkness!

Black frost. The earth is hard, the air bitter to the taste. Your stars are joined into evil signs.

With petrified steps you stamp along the rail embankment, with round eyes, like a soldier storming a black bulwark. Avanti!

Bitter snow and moon!

A red wolf strangled by an angel. Striding on, your legs ring out like blue ice and a smile full of mourning and pride has petrified your countenance and your brow grows pale from the rapture of the frost;

or it is bent in silence over the sleep of a guard who sank to earth inside his wooden hut.

Frost and smoke. A white shirt made of stars scorches the burdened shoulders and God's vultures tear apart your metallic heart.

O the stony hill. Silent and lost to oblivion the chill body melts in the silver snow.

Black is sleep. The ear long follows the traces of the stars in the ice.

On awakening, the village bells tolled. Through the eastern gate roseate day appeared all in silver.

IN VENEDIG

Stille in nächtigem Zimmer.
Silbern flackert der Leuchter
Vor dem singenden Odem
Des Einsamen;
Zaubrisches Rosengewölk.

Schwärzlicher Fliegenschwarm
Verdunkelt den steinernen Raum
Und es starrt von der Qual
Des goldenen Tags das Haupt
Des Heimatlosen.

Reglos nachtet das Meer.
Stern und schwärzliche Fahrt
Entschwand am Kanal.
Kind, dein kränkliches Lächeln
Folgte mir leise im Schlaf.

VORHÖLLE

An herbstlichen Mauern, es suchen Schatten dort
Am Hügel das tönende Gold
Weidende Abendwolken
In der Ruh verdorrter Platanen.
Dunklere Tränen odmet diese Zeit,
Verdammnis, da des Träumers Herz
Überfließt von purpurner Abendröte,
Der Schwermut der rauchenden Stadt;
Dem Schreitenden nachweht goldene Kühle,
Dem Fremdling, vom Friedhof,
Als folgte im Schatten ein zarter Leichnam.

IN VENICE

Silence in nocturnal chamber.
Silver the candelabra flickers
Before the singing breath
Of the lonesome man;
Magical roseate clouds.

Blackish swarming of flies
Darkens the stony room
And from the torment of a golden day
The head of the homeless one
Starkly stares.

Motionless sea turns night.
Star and blackish voyage
Faded beside the canal.
Beloved, your sickly smile
Softly pursued me in sleep.

LIMBO

By autumnal walls, there shadows seek
Resonant gold by the hill,
Pasturing evening clouds
In the peace of desiccated planes.
This age breathes darker tears,
Damnation, when the dreamer's heart
Overflows with purple sunset,
With the melancholy of the smoking town;
A golden chill wafts after the stroller,
The stranger, from the graveyard,
Like a gentle corpse that follows in the shadows.

Leise läutet der steinerne Bau;
Der Garten der Waisen, das dunkle Spital,
Ein rotes Schiff am Kanal.
Träumend steigen und sinken im Dunkel
Verwesende Menschen
Und aus schwärzlichen Toren
Treten Engel mit kalten Stirnen hervor;
Bläue, die Todesklagen der Mütter.
Es rollt durch ihr langes Haar,
Ein feuriges Rad, der runde Tag
Der Erde Qual ohne Ende.

In kühlen Zimmern ohne Sinn
Modert Gerät, mit knöchernen Händen
Tastet im Blau nach Märchen
Unheilige Kindheit,
Benagt die fette Ratte Tür und Truh,
Ein Herz
Erstarrt in schneeiger Stille.
Nachhallen die purpurnen Flüche
Des Hungers in faulendem Dunkel,
Die schwarzen Schwerter der Lüge,
Als schlüge zusammen ein ehernes Tor.

DIE SONNE

Täglich kommt die gelbe Sonne über den Hügel.
Schön ist der Wald, das dunkle Tier,
Der Mensch; Jäger oder Hirt.

Rötlich steigt im grünen Weiher der Fisch.
Unter dem runden Himmel
Fährt der Fischer leise im blauen Kahn.

Langsam reift die Traube, das Korn.
Wenn sich stille der Tag neigt,
Ist ein Gutes und Böses bereitet.

Wenn es Nacht wird,
Hebt der Wanderer leise die schweren Lider;
Sonne aus finsterer Schlucht bricht.

The building of stone softly rings;
The orphans' garden, the dark hospital,
A red ship by the canal.
Dreaming there rise and fall in darkness
Putrefying people
And from blackish gateways
Rise angels with cold brows;
Blueness, the mothers' mournful laments.
Through their long hair rolls
A wheel of fire, the round day,
Earth's torment without end.

In cool chambers without sense
Equipment rots, with skeletal hands
Unholy childhood
Probes in blueness for fairytales,
The fat rat gnaws at door and trunk,
A heart
Grows rigid in snowy silence.
The purple curses of hunger
Echo in rotting gloom,
The black swords of lying,
Like the slamming of bronze doors.

THE SUN

Daily the yellow sun comes over the hill.
Lovely the forest, the dark animal,
Man himself; hunter or shepherd.

Reddish the fish rises in the green pond.
Beneath the round heavens
The fisherman drifts quietly in the blue boat.

Slowly the grape ripens, the corn.
When day silently moves to its close,
Something good and evil is prepared.

When night falls,
The wanderer quietly raises heavy eyelids;
Sun breaks from a gloomy abyss.

GESANG EINER GEFANGENEN AMSEL

Für Ludwig von Ficker

Dunkler Odem im grünen Gezweig.
Blaue Blümchen umschweben das Antlitz
Des Einsamen, den goldnen Schritt
Ersterbend unter dem Ölbaum.
Aufflattert mit trunknem Flügel die Nacht.
So leise blutet Demut,
Tau, der langsam tropft vom blühenden Dorn.
Strahlender Arme Erbarmen
Umfängt ein brechendes Herz.

SOMMER

Am Abend schweigt die Klage
Des Kuckucks im Wald.
Tiefer neigt sich das Korn,
Der rote Mohn.

Schwarzes Gewitter droht
Über dem Hügel.
Das alte Lied der Grille
Erstirbt im Feld.

Nimmer regt sich das Laub
Der Kastanie.
Auf der Wendeltreppe
Rauscht dein Kleid.

Stille leuchtet die Kerze
Im dunklen Zimmer;
Eine silberne Hand
Löschte sie aus;

Windstille, sternlose Nacht.

SONG OF A CAPTIVE BLACKBIRD

For Ludwig von Ficker

Dark breath in green branches.
Little blue flowers enfold the solitary man's
Countenance, the golden tread
Dying away under the olive tree.
Night flutters up on drunken wing.
Humility bleeds so softly,
Dew that slowly drips from the blossoming thorn.
Compassion of radiant arms
Embraces a breaking heart.

SUMMER

At evening the cuckoo's lament
In the wood is silent.
The corn stoops lower,
The red poppy.

Black storms threaten
Above the hill.
The cricket's ancient song
Dies in the field.

The leaves of the chestnut
Never stir.
On the winding stair
Your dress rustles.

The candle shines in silence
In the dark chamber;
A silver hand
Extinguishes it;

Deep calm, starless night.

Der grüne Sommer ist so leise
Geworden, dein kristallenes Antlitz.
Am Abendweiher starben die Blumen,
Ein erschrockener Amselruf.

Vergebliche Hoffnung des Lebens. Schon rüstet
Zur Reise sich die Schwalbe im Haus
Und die Sonne versinkt am Hügel;
Schon winkt zur Sternenreise die Nacht.

Stille der Dörfer; es tönen rings
Die verlassenen Wälder. Herz,
Neige dich nun liebender
Über die ruhige Schläferin.

Der grüne Sommer ist so leise
Geworden und es läutet der Schritt
Des Fremdlings durch die silberne Nacht.
Gedächte ein blaues Wild seines Pfads,

Des Wohllauts seiner geistlichen Jahre!

JAHR

Dunkle Stille der Kindheit. Unter grünenden Eschen
Weidet die Sanftmut bläulichen Blickes; goldene Ruh.
Ein Dunkles entzückt der Duft der Veilchen; schwankende Ähren
Im Abend, Samen und die goldenen Schatten der Schwermut.
Balken behaut der Zimmermann; im dämmernden Grund
Mahlt die Mühle; im Hasellaub wölbt sich ein purpurner Mund,
Männliches rot über schweigende Wasser geneigt.
Leise ist der Herbst, der Geist des Waldes; goldene Wolke
Folgt dem Einsamen, der schwarze Schatten des Enkels.
Neige in steinernem Zimmer; unter alten Zypressen
Sind der Tränen nächtige Bilder zum Quell versammelt;
Goldenes Auge des Anbeginns, dunkle Geduld des Endes.

The green summer has grown so quiet,
Your crystalline countenance.
By the evening pond the flowers died,
A blackbird's startled cry.

Vain hope of life. At home the swallow
Now prepares for its journey
And the sun sinks down by the hill;
Night now beckons on its journey to the stars.

Silence of hamlets; all around the deserted woods
Resound. Heart,
Stoop now with greater love
Over the tranquil girl asleep.

The green summer has grown so quiet
And the stranger's tread rings
Through the silver night.
Would that a blue prey were mindful of its way,

The harmony of its spiritual years!

YEAR

Dark silence of childhood. Under young green ashtrees
Meekness broods with bluish glance; golden peace.
A dark thing delights in the fragrance of violets; swaying ears of corn
At evening, seeds and the golden shades of melancholy.
Beams are hewn by the carpenter; in the twilit vale
The mill grinds; a scarlet mouth swells amid hazel leaves,
Manly red bowed over silent waters.
Quiet is the autumn, the spirit of the forest; golden cloud
Follows the solitary man, the grandson's black shadow.
Decline in the room of stone; the night images of tears
Are gathered at the source under ancient cypresses;
Golden eye of inception, dark patience of the end.

ABENDLAND

Vierte Fassung

Else Lasker-Schüler in Verehrung

1

Mond, als träte ein Totes
Aus blauer Höhle,
Und es fallen der Blüten
Viele über den Felsenpfad.
Silbern weint ein Krankes
Am Abendweiher,
Auf schwarzem Kahn
Hinüberstarben Liebende.

Oder es läuten die Schritte
Elis' durch den Hain
Den hyazinthenen
Wieder verhallend unter Eichen.
O des Knaben Gestalt
Geformt aus kristallenen Tränen,
Nächtigen Schatten.
Zackige Blitze erhellen die Schläfe
Die immerkühle,
Wenn am grünenden Hügel
Frühlingsgewitter ertönt.

2

So leise sind die grünen Wälder
Unsrer Heimat,
Die kristallne Woge
Hinsterbend an verfallner Mauer
Und wir haben im Schlaf geweint;
Wandern mit zögernden Schritten
An der dornigen Hecke hin
Singende im Abendsommer,
In heiliger Ruh
Des fern verstrahlenden Weinbergs;
Schatten nun im kühlen Schoß

Fourth version

Dedicated to Else Lasker-Schüler

1

Moon, as if a dead thing
Emerged from a blue cavern,
And manifold blossoms fall
Upon the rocky path.
All silver a sick creature
Weeps by the evening pond,
Upon a black barge
Lovers crossing died.

Or Elis's footsteps
Ring through the grove
Hyacinth-filled
Dying away again under oaks.
O the figure of the boy
Fashioned from crystal tears,
Shadows of night.
Jagged flashes of lightning illumine
The ever cool brow
When Spring storms resound
By the fresh green hill.

2

So quiet are the green woods
Of our homeland,
The crystalline wave
Dying away by the ruined wall,
And we wept in sleep;
Wandering with timid steps
Down past the thorny thicket,
Singers in summer's eve,
In the sacred peace
Of the far resplendent vineyard;
Shadows now in the cool womb

Der Nacht, trauernde Adler.
So leise schließt ein mondener Strahl
Die purpurnen Male der Schwermut.

3

Ihr großen Städte
Steinern aufgebaut
In der Ebene!
So sprachlos folgt
Der Heimatlose
Mit dunkler Stirne dem Wind,
Kahlen Bäumen am Hügel.
Ihr weithin dämmernden Ströme!
Gewaltig ängstet
Schaurige Abendröte
Im Sturmgewölk.
Ihr sterbenden Völker!
Bleiche Woge
Zerschellend am Strande der Nacht,
Fallende Sterne.

FRÜHLING DER SEELE II

Aufschrei im Schlaf; durch schwarze Gassen stürzt der Wind,
Das Blau des Frühlings winkt durch brechendes Geäst,
Purpurner Nachttau und es erlöschen rings die Sterne.
Grünlich dämmert der Fluß, silbern die alten Alleen
Und die Türme der Stadt. O sanfte Trunkenheit
Im gleitenden Kahn und die dunklen Rufe der Amsel
In kindlichen Gärten. Schon lichtet sich der rosige Flor.

Feierlich rauschen die Wasser. O die feuchten Schatten der Au,
Das schreitende Tier; Grünendes, Blütengezweig
Rührt die kristallene Stirne; schimmernder Schaukelkahn.
Leise tönt die Sonne im Rosengewölk am Hügel.
Groß ist die Stille des Tannenwalds, die ernsten Schatten am Fluß.

Of night, grief-stricken eagles.
As gently does a moonlit beam close
The scarlet scars of melancholy.

3

You great cities
Reared of stone
In the plains!
Speechless with dark brow
The homeless man
Follows the wind,
Bare trees by the hillside.
You far-flung fading rivers!
Fearful sunsets
In tempest clouds
Inspire mighty dread.
You dying nations!
Pallid wave
Breaking upon night's shore,
Falling stars.

SPRINGTIME OF THE SOUL II

Cry out in sleep; the wind tears through black streets,
Spring's blueness beckons through breaking boughs,
Scarlet night dew and round about the stars go out.
Greenish the river dusks, silver the ancient avenues
And towers of the city. O gentle ecstasy
In the gliding boat and the dark calls of the blackbird
In childhood gardens. Now the roseate bloom clears.

Gravely the waters murmur. O the moist shades of the meadow,
Animals striding; greenery, blossomy branches
Touch the crystalline brow; shimmering rocking-boat.
Quiet the sun rings in roseate mists by the hill.
Great is the silence of the pine forest, the grave shadows by
    the stream.

Reinheit! Reinheit! Wo sind die furchtbaren Pfade des Todes,
Des grauen steinernen Schweigens, die Felsen der Nacht
Und die friedlosen Schatten? Strahlender Sonnenabgrund.

Schwester, da ich dich fand an einsamer Lichtung
Des Waldes und Mittag war und groß das Schweigen des Tiers;
Weiße unter wilder Eiche, und es blühte silbern der Dorn.
Gewaltiges Sterben und die singende Flamme im Herzen.

Dunkler umfließen die Wasser die schönen Spiele der Fische.
Stunde der Trauer, schweigender Anblick der Sonne;
Es ist die Seele ein Fremdes auf Erden. Geistlich dämmert
Bläue über dem verhauenen Wald und es läutet
Lange eine dunkle Glocke im Dorf; friedlich Geleit.
Stille blüht die Myrthe über den weißen Lidern des Toten.

Leise tönen die Wasser im sinkenden Nachmittag
Und es grünet dunkler die Wildnis am Ufer, Freude im rosigen Wind;
Der sanfte Gesang des Bruders am Abendhügel.

IM DUNKEL

Zweite Fassung

Es schweigt die Seele den blauen Frühling.
Unter feuchtem Abendgezweig
Sank in Schauern die Stirne den Liebenden.

O das grünende Kreuz. In dunklem Gespräch
Erkannten sich Mann und Weib.
An kahler Mauer
Wandelt mit seinen Gestirnen der Einsame.

Über die mondbeglänzten Wege des Walds
Sank die Wildnis
Vergessener Jagden; Blick der Bläue
Aus verfallenen Felsen bricht.

Pureness! Pureness! Where are the terrible paths of death,
Of grey stony silence, the cliffs of night
And the shadows without peace? Radiant sunny abyss.

Sister, when I found you by a lonely clearing
Of the forest and it was noon and great the silence of animal life;
White ones beneath wild oak, and silver the thorn flowered.
Mighty decease and the singing flame in the heart.

Darker the waters flow about the lovely games of the fish.
Hour of grieving, silent aspect of the sun;
The soul is a stranger to earth. Blueness lingers
In spirit above the denuded forest and in the village
A dark bell tolls long; peaceful attendance.
Tranquil the myrtle flowers above the white eyelids of the dead.

Quiet the waters ring in the afternoon's decline
And the wilderness grows green more darkly by the shore; joy in
    the roseate breeze;
Brother's gentle song by the evening hill.

IN THE DARK

Second version

The soul speaks silence to blue springtime.
Under moist evening branches
Shuddering the lovers' brow sank low.

O the green-sprouting Cross. In dark converse
Man and Woman knew each other.
By the naked wall
The solitary man walks with his stars.

Over the moonlit paths of the forest
The wasteland of forgotten hunts
Sank low; glance of blueness
Breaks from derelict rocks.

GESANG DES ABGESCHIEDENEN

An Karl Borromaeus Heinrich

Voll Harmonien ist der Flug der Vögel. Es haben die grünen Wälder
Am Abend sich zu stilleren Hütten versammelt;
Die kristallenen Weiden des Rehs.
Dunkles besänftigt das Plätschern des Bachs, die feuchten Schatten

Und die Blumen des Sommers, die schön im Winde läuten.
Schon dämmert die Stirne dem sinnenden Menschen.

Und es leuchtet ein Lämpchen, das Gute, in seinem Herzen
Und der Frieden des Mahls; denn geheiligt ist Brot und Wein
Von Gottes Händen, und es schaut aus nächtigen Augen
Stille dich der Bruder an, daß er ruhe von dorniger Wanderschaft.
O das Wohnen in der beseelten Bläue der Nacht.

Liebend auch umfängt das Schweigen im Zimmer die Schatten der Alten,
Die purpurnen Martern, Klage eines großen Geschlechts,
Das fromm nun hingeht im einsamen Enkel.

Denn strahlender immer erwacht aus schwarzen Minuten des Wahnsinns
Der Duldende an versteinerter Schwelle
Und es umfängt ihn gewaltig die kühle Bläue und die leuchtende Neige
    des Herbstes,

Das stille Haus und die Sagen des Waldes,
Maß und Gesetz und die mondenen Pfade der Abgeschiedenen.

TRAUM UND UMNACHTUNG

Am Abend ward zum Greis der Vater; in dunklen Zimmern versteinerte das
Antlitz der Mutter und auf dem Knaben lastete der Fluch des entarteten Ge-
schlechts. Manchmal erinnerte er sich seiner Kindheit, erfüllt von Krankheit,
Schrecken und Finsternis, verschwiegener Spiele im Sternengarten, oder daß
er die Ratten fütterte im dämmernden Hof. Aus blauem Spiegel trat die
schmale Gestalt der Schwester und er stürzte wie tot ins Dunkel. Nachts
brach sein Mund gleich einer roten Frucht auf und die Sterne erglänzten über
seiner sprachlosen Trauer. Seine Träume erfüllten das alte Haus der Väter.
Am Abend ging er gerne über den verfallenen Friedhof, oder er besah in
dämmernder Totenkammer die Leichen, die grünen Flecken der Verwesung

SONG OF THE RECLUSE

To Karl Borromaeus Heinrich

The flight of birds is full of harmonies. The green woods have gathered
At evening to quieter tabernacles;
The crystalline pastures of the deer.
A darkness mellows the plash of the brook, the moist shadows

And the flowers of summer that ring lovely in the wind.
The brow of pensive Man now gathers gloom.

And a little lamp, Goodness, shines within his heart
And the peace of the meal; for blessed are bread and wine
By the hands of God, and your brother beholds you
In silence with night-dark eyes, that he find rest from thorny journeying.
O to dwell in the bliss-filled blueness of night.

Lovingly too does night embrace the shades of the aged in the room,
The scarlet torments, lament of a great lineage
That now piously fades in the solitary grandson.

For ever more radiantly the sufferer wakes from bleak minutes of madness
On the petrified threshold
And cool blueness embraces him with might and the lambent decline of
    the autumn.

The silent house and the legends of the forest,
Just measure and law and the moonglade paths of the recluse.

DREAM AND DERANGEMENT

At evening Father became an aged man; in dark rooms Mother's counten-
ance turned to stone and the curse of the degenerate race weighed upon the
youth. At times he remembered his childhood filled with sickness, terrors
and darkness, secretive games in the starlit garden, or that he fed the rats in
the twilit yard. Out of a blue mirror stepped the slender form of his sister and
he fled as if dead into the dark. At night his mouth broke open like a red fruit
and the stars grew bright above his speechless sorrow. His dreams filled the
ancient house of his forefathers. At evening he loved to walk across the
derelict graveyard, or he perused the corpses in a dusky death-chamber, the
green spots of decay upon their lovely hands. By the convent gate he begged

auf ihren schönen Händen. An der Pforte des Klosters bat er um ein Stück Brot; der Schatten eines Rappen sprang aus dem Dunkel und erschreckte ihn. Wenn er in seinem kühlen Bette lag, überkamen ihn unsägliche Tränen. Aber es war niemand, der die Hand auf seine Stirne gelegt hätte. Wenn der Herbst kam, ging er, ein Hellseher, in brauner Au. O, die Stunden wilder Verzückung, die Abende am grünen Fluß, die Jagden. O, die Seele, die leise das Lied des vergilbten Rohrs sang; feurige Frömmigkeit. Stille sah er und lang in die Sternenaugen der Kröte, befühlte mit erschauernden Händen die Kühle des alten Steins und besprach die ehrwürdige Sage des blauen Quells. O, die silbernen Fische und die Früchte, die von verkrüppelten Bäumen fielen. Die Akkorde seiner Schritte erfüllten ihn mit Stolz und Menschenverachtung. Am Heimweg traf er ein unbewohntes Schloß. Verfallene Götter standen im Garten, hintrauernd am Abend. Ihm aber schien: hier lebte ich vergessene Jahre. Ein Orgelchoral erfüllte ihn mit Gottes Schauern. Aber in dunkler Höhle verbrachte er seine Tage, log und stahl und verbarg sich, ein flammender Wolf, vor dem weißen Antlitz der Mutter. O, die Stunde, da er mit steinernem Munde im Sternengarten hinsank, der Schatten des Mörders über ihn kam. Mit purpurner Stirne ging er ins Moor und Gottes Zorn züchtigte seine metallenen Schultern; o, die Birken im Sturm, das dunkle Getier, das seine umnachteten Pfade mied. Haß verbrannte sein Herz, Wollust, da er im grünenden Sommergarten dem schweigenden Kind Gewalt tat, in dem strahlenden sein umnachtetes Antlitz erkannte. Weh, des Abends am Fenster, da aus purpurnen Blumen, ein gräulich Gerippe, der Tod trat. O, ihr Türme und Glocken; und die Schatten der Nacht fielen steinern auf ihn.

Niemand liebte ihn. Sein Haupt verbrannte Lüge und Unzucht in dämmernden Zimmern. Das blaue Rauschen eines Frauengewandes ließ ihn zur Säule erstarren und in der Tür stand die nächtige Gestalt seiner Mutter. Zu seinen Häupten erhob sich der Schatten des Bösen. O, ihr Nächte und Sterne. Am Abend ging er mit dem Krüppel am Berge hin; auf eisigem Gipfel lag der rosige Glanz der Abendröte und sein Herz läutete leise in der Dämmerung. Schwer sanken die stürmischen Tannen über sie und der rote Jäger trat aus dem Wald. Da es Nacht ward, zerbrach kristallen sein Herz und die Finsternis schlug seine Stirne. Unter kahlen Eichbäumen erwürgte er mit eisigen Händen eine wilde Katze. Klagend zur Rechten erschien die weiße Gestalt eines Engels, und es wuchs im Dunkel der Schatten des Krüppels. Er aber hob einen Stein und warf ihn nach jenem, daß er heulend floh, und seufzend verging im Schatten des Baums das sanfte Antlitz des Engels. Lange lag er auf steinigem Acker und sah staunend das goldene Zelt der Sterne. Von Fledermäusen gejagt, stürzte er fort ins Dunkel. Atemlos trat er ins verfallene

for a piece of bread; the shadow of a black horse sprang out of the darkness and startled him. When he lay in his cool bed, he was overcome by indescribable tears. But there was nobody who might have laid a hand on his brow. When autumn came he walked, a visionary, in brown meadows. O, the hours of wild ecstasy, the evenings by the green stream, the hunts. O, the soul that softly sang the song of the withered reed; fiery piety. Silent and long he gazed into the starry eyes of the toad, felt with thrilling hands the coolness of ancient stone and invoked the time-honoured legend of the blue spring. O, the silver fishes and the fruit that fell from crippled trees. The chiming chords of his footsteps filled him with pride and contempt for mankind. Along his homeward path he came upon a deserted castle. Ruined gods stood in the garden sorrowfully at eventide. Yet to him it seemed: here I have lived forgotten years. An organ chorale filled him with the thrill of God. But he spent his days in a dark cave, lied and stole and hid himself, a flaming wolf, from his mother's white countenance. O, that hour when he sank low with stony mouth in the starlit garden, the shadow of the murderer fell upon him. With scarlet brow he entered the moor and the wrath of God chastised his metal shoulders; O, the birches in the storm, the dark creatures that shunned his deranged paths. Hatred scorched his heart, rapture, when he did violence to the silent child in the fresh green summer garden, recognized in the radiant his deranged countenance. Woe, that evening by the window, when a horrid skeleton, Death, emerged from scarlet flowers. O, you towers and bells; and the shadows of night fell as stone upon him.

No one loved him. His head burnt up lies and licentiousness in twilit rooms. The blue rustling of a woman's dress turned him into a pillar of stone and in the doorway stood the night-dark figure of his mother. Over his head reared the shadow of Evil. O, you nights and stars. At evening he walked by the mountain with the cripple; upon the icy summit lay the roseate gleam of sunset and his heart rang quietly in the twilight. The stormy pines sank heavily over them and the red huntsman stepped out of the forest. When night fell, his heart broke like crystal and darkness beat his brow. Beneath bare oak trees with icy hands he strangled a wild cat. At the right hand appeared the white form of an angel lamenting, and in the darkness the cripple's shadow grew. But he took up a stone and threw it at the man that he fled howling, and sighing the gentle countenance of the angel vanished in the shadow of the tree. Long he lay on the stony field and gazed astonished at the golden canopy of the stars. Pursued by bats he plunged into darkness. Breathless he stepped into the derelict house. In the courtyard he, a wild animal, drank from the blue waters of the well till he felt the chill. Feverish he

Haus. Im Hof trank er, ein wildes Tier, von den blauen Wassern des Brunnens, bis ihn fror. Fiebernd saß er auf der eisigen Stiege, rasend gen Gott, daß er stürbe. O, das graue Antlitz des Schreckens, da er die runden Augen über einer Taube zerschnittener Kehle auf hob. Huschend über fremde Stiegen begegnete er einem Judenmädchen und er griff nach ihrem schwarzen Haar und er nahm ihren Mund. Feindliches folgte ihm durch finstere Gassen und sein Ohr zerriß ein eisernes Klirren. An herbstlichen Mauern folgte er, ein Mesnerknabe, stille dem schweigenden Priester; unter verdorrten Bäumen atmete er trunken den Scharlach jenes ehrwürdigen Gewands. O, die verfallene Scheibe der Sonne. Süße Martern verzehrten sein Fleisch. In einem verödeten Durchhaus erschien ihm starrend von Unrat seine blutende Gestalt. Tiefer liebte er die erhabenen Werke des Steins; den Turm, der mit höllischen Fratzen nächtlich den blauen Sternenhimmel stürmt; das kühle Grab, darin des Menschen feuriges Herz bewahrt ist. Weh, der unsäglichen Schuld, die jenes kundtut. Aber da er Glühendes sinnend den herbstlichen Fluß hinabging unter kahlen Bäumen hin, erschien in härenem Mantel ihm, ein flammender Dämon, die Schwester. Beim Erwachen erloschen zu ihren Häuptern die Sterne.

O des verfluchten Geschlechts. Wenn in befleckten Zimmern jegliches Schicksal vollendet ist, tritt mit modernden Schritten der Tod in das Haus. O, daß draußen Frühling wäre und im blühenden Baum ein lieblicher Vogel sänge. Aber gräulich verdorrt das spärliche Grün an den Fenstern der Nächtlichen und es sinnen die blutenden Herzen noch Böses. O, die dämmernden Frühlingswege des Sinnenden. Gerechter erfreut ihn die blühende Hecke, die junge Saat des Landmanns und der singende Vogel, Gottes sanftes Geschöpf; die Abendglocke und die schöne Gemeine der Menschen. Daß er seines Schicksals vergäße und des dornigen Stachels. Frei ergrünt der Bach, wo silbern wandelt sein Fuß, und ein sagender Baum rauscht über dem umnachteten Haupt ihm. Also hebt er mit schmächtiger Hand die Schlange, und in feurigen Tränen schmolz ihm das Herz hin. Erhaben ist das Schweigen des Walds, ergrüntes Dunkel und das moosige Getier, aufflatternd, wenn es Nacht wird. O der Schauer, da jegliches seine Schuld weiß, dornige Pfade geht. Also fand er im Dornenbusch die weiße Gestalt des Kindes, blutend nach dem Mantel seines Bräutigams. Er aber stand vergraben in sein stählernes Haar stumm und leidend vor ihr. O die strahlenden Engel, die der purpurne Nachtwind zerstreute. Nachtlang wohnte er in kristallener Höhle und der Aussatz wuchs silbern auf seiner Stirne. Ein Schatten ging er den Saumpfad hinab unter herbstlichen Sternen. Schnee fiel, und blaue Finsternis erfüllte das Haus. Eines Blinden klang die harte Stimme des Vaters und

sat on the icy steps, raging against God that he was dying. O, the grey countenance of terror, as he raised his round eyes over the slit throat of a dove. Hastening over strange stairways he encountered a Jewish girl and clutched at her black hair and he took her mouth. A hostile force followed him through gloomy streets and an iron clash rent his ear. By autumnal walls he, now an altar boy, quietly followed the silent priest; under arid trees in ecstasy he breathed the scarlet of that venerated garment. O, the derelict disc of the sun. Sweet torments consumed his flesh. In a deserted half-way house a bleeding figure appeared to him rigid with refuse. He loved the sublime works of stone more deeply; the tower which assails the starry blue firmament with fiendish grimace; the cool grave in which Man's fiery heart is preserved. Woe to the unspeakable guilt which declares all this. But since he walked down along the autumn river pondering glowing things beneath bare trees, a flaming demon in a mantle of hair appeared to him, his sister. On awakening, the stars about their heads went out.

O, the accursed race. When every manner of destiny is accomplished in defiled rooms, Death enters the house with mouldering steps. O, that it were spring outside and that a sweet bird might sing in the blossoming tree. But the sparse greenery withers greyly by the windows of creatures of night and hearts that bleed still contemplate evil. O, the twilit spring paths of the pensive man. The blossoming hedgerow delights him more righteously, the countryman's young corn and the singing bird, God's gentle creature; the evening bell and the lovely fellowship of mankind. That he might only forget his destiny and the pricking thorn. Freely the brook shows green where in silver he sets his foot and a rumouring tree rustles above his night-shaded head. Then he lifts the serpent with frail hand and his heart melted away in fiery tears. Sublime is the silence of the forest, darkness grown green and the mossy creatures fluttering aloft when night falls. O, the thrill when each knows its own guilt, travels the thorny paths. Thus did he find the white form of the child in the thorn bush, bleeding after the cloak of its bridegroom. Yet he stood before her buried in his steely hair, mute and suffering. O, the radiant angels scattered by the purple night winds. Long nights did he dwell in a crystal cave and leprosy grew all silvery upon his brow. A shadow, he walked down the boundary path beneath autumnal stars. Snow fell and the blue darkness filled the house. As a blind man's, Father's harsh voice resounded and called up dread. Woe, the bowed appearance of women. Beneath petrified hands fruit and implements mouldered to the appalled race. A wolf devoured the first-born and my sisters fled into dark gardens to skeletal old men. A deranged seer, that man sang by the derelict walls and

beschwor das Grauen. Weh der gebeugten Erscheinung der Frauen. Unter erstarrten Händen verfielen Frucht und Gerät dem entsetzten Geschlecht. Ein Wolf zerriß das Erstgeborene und die Schwestern flohen in dunkle Gärten zu knöchernen Greisen. Ein umnachteter Seher sang jener an verfallenen Mauern und seine Stimme verschlang Gottes Wind. O die Wollust des Todes. O ihr Kinder eines dunklen Geschlechts. Silbern schimmern die bösen Blumen des Bluts an jenes Schläfe, der kalte Mond in seinen zerbrochenen Augen. O, der Nächtlichen; o, der Verfluchten.

Tief ist der Schlummer in dunklen Giften, erfüllt von Sternen und dem weißen Antlitz der Mutter, dem steinernen. Bitter ist der Tod, die Kost der Schuldbeladenen; in dem braunen Geäst des Stamms zerfielen grinsend die irdenen Gesichter. Aber leise sang jener im grünen Schatten des Hollunders, da er aus bösen Träumen erwachte; süßer Gespiele nahte ihm ein rosiger Engel, daß er, ein sanftes Wild, zur Nacht hinschlummerte; und er sah das Sternenantlitz der Reinheit. Golden sanken die Sonnenblumen über den Zaun des Gartens, da es Sommer ward. O, der Fleiß der Bienen und das grüne Laub des Nußbaums; die vorüberziehenden Gewitter. Silbern blühte der Mohn auch, trug in grüner Kapsel unsere nächtigen Sternenträume. O, wie stille war das Haus, als der Vater ins Dunkel hinging. Purpurn reifte die Frucht am Baum und der Gärtner rührte die harten Hände; o die härenen Zeichen in strahlender Sonne. Aber stille trat am Abend der Schatten des Toten in den trauernden Kreis der Seinen und es klang kristallen sein Schritt über die grünende Wiese vorm Wald. Schweigende versammelten sich jene am Tisch; Sterbende brachen sie mit wächsernen Händen das Brot, das blutende. Weh der steinernen Augen der Schwester, da beim Mahle ihr Wahnsinn auf die nächtige Stirne des Bruders trat, der Mutter unter leidenden Händen das Brot zu Stein ward. O der Verwesten, da sie mit silbernen Zungen die Hölle schwiegen. Also erloschen die Lampen im kühlen Gemach und aus purpurnen Masken sahen schweigend sich die leidenden Menschen an. Die Nacht lang rauschte ein Regen und erquickte die Flur. In dorniger Wildnis folgte der Dunkle den vergilbten Pfaden im Korn, dem Lied der Lerche und der sanften Stille des grünen Gezweigs, daß er Frieden fände. O, ihr Dörfer und moosigen Stufen, glühender Anblick. Aber beinern schwanken die Schritte über schlafende Schlangen am Waldsaum und das Ohr folgt immer dem rasenden Schrei des Geiers. Steinige Öde fand er am Abend, Geleite eines Toten in das dunkle Haus des Vaters. Purpurne Wolke umwölkte sein Haupt, daß er schweigend über sein eigenes Blut und Bildnis herfiel, ein mondenes Antlitz; steinern ins Leere hinsank, da in zerbrochenem Spiegel, ein sterbender Jüngling, die Schwester erschien; die Nacht das verfluchte Geschlecht verschlang.

God's wind consumed his voice. O ecstasy of death. O you children of a midnight race. All silver the evil flowers of the blood shimmer about that man's brow, the cold moon within his broken eyes. O, the creatures of night; O, those who are accursed.

Deep is the slumber in dark poisons, replete with stars and Mother's white countenance, one of stone. Bitter is death, the food of the heavy laden; in the brown branches of the stem the earthen faces crumbled grinning. But that man sang quietly in the green shade of the elder when he awoke from evil dreams; sweet plaything, a rosy angel approached him, so that he, a gentle creature of the wild, fell asleep toward night; and he saw the starry countenance of purity. Golden the sunflowers sank down over the garden fence when summer came. O, the diligence of the bees and the green foliage of the walnut tree; the passing storms. Silver, the poppy also bloomed, bore our night dreams of the stars in a green capsule. O how silent was the house when Father passed into the darkness. Purple, the fruit of the tree ripened and the gardener bestirred his hard hands; o the harsh signs in the radiant sun. Yet silently the dead man's shade entered the grieving circle of his own and his step rang as crystal over the fresh green meadow before the forest. Silent beings, they gathered about the table; dying beings, they broke the bread which bled with waxen hands. Woe, the stony eyes of sister, when at the meal her madness entered upon the night-dark brow of her brother, under Mother's suffering hands the bread turned to stone. O to those perished, when they with silver tongues kept Hell in silence. Then the lamps went out in the cool chamber and through purple masks the suffering humans looked at one another in silence. All night long the rain plashed and refreshed the earth. Amidst thorny wilderness the man of darkness followed the yellowed paths through the corn, the lark's song and the gentle silence of green branches, that he might find peace. O, you villages and mossy steps, glowing aspect. But the footsteps waver bonily over sleeping snakes at the forest edge and the ear ever follows the rabid cry of the vulture. At evening, he came upon stony wasteland, escort to a dead man into the dark house of his father. A purple cloud wreathed his brow, that he fell upon his own blood and image in silence, a moon-like countenance; stonily sank into a void, when in a broken mirror there appeared a dying youth, his sister; night swallowed up the accursed race.

IN HELLBRUNN

Wieder folgend der blauen Klage des Abends
Am Hügel hin, am Frühlingsweiher
Als schwebten darüber die Schatten lange Verstorbener,
Die Schatten der Kirchenfürsten, edler Frauen –
Schon blühen ihre Blumen, die ernsten Veilchen
Im Abendgrund, rauscht des blauen Quells
Kristallne Woge. So geistlich ergrünen
Die Eichen über den vergessenen Pfaden der Toten,
Die goldene Wolke über dem Weiher.

DAS HERZ

Das wilde Herz ward weiß am Wald;
O dunkle Angst
Des Todes, so das Gold
In grauer Wolke starb.
Novemberabend.
Am kahlen Tor am Schlachthaus stand
Der armen Frauen Schar;
In jeden Korb
Fiel faules Fleisch und Eingeweid;
Verfluchte Kost!

Des Abends blaue Taube
Brachte nicht Versöhnung.
Dunkler Trompetenruf
Durchfuhr der Ulmen
Nasses Goldlaub,
Eine zerfetzte Fahne
Vom Blute rauchend,

IN HELLBRUNN

Following once more the evening's blue lament
Along the hill, along the springtime pond –
As if the shades of those long dead should hover,
The shades of princes of the church, of noble women –
The flowers now blossom, the grave violets
In evening vale, the crystalline wave
Of the blue spring murmurs. So sacredly the oaks
Grow green over forgotten paths of the deceased,
The golden cloud above the pond.

THE HEART

The wild heart grew white by the forest;
O darksome fear
Of death, so died
The gold in a grey cloud.
November evening
By naked gate of slaughterhouse there stood
Impoverished women's little band;
Into each basket
Fell foul flesh and entrails;
Cursed fare!

Evening's blue dove
Brought no propitiation.
Dark trumpeting
Surged through the elms'
Wet golden leaf,
A ragged banner
Smoking with blood,

Daß in wilder Schwermut
Hinlauscht ein Mann.
O! ihr ehernen Zeiten
Begraben dort im Abendrot.

Aus dunklem Hausflur trat
Die goldne Gestalt
Der Jünglingin
Umgeben von bleichen Monden,
Herbstlicher Hofstaat,
Zerknickten schwarze Tannen
Im Nachtsturm,
Die steile Festung.
O Herz
Hinüberschimmernd in schneeige Kühle.

DER SCHLAF

Zweite Fassung

Verflucht ihr dunklen Gifte,
Weißer Schlaf!
Dieser höchst seltsame Garten
Dämmernder Bäume
Erfüllt von Schlangen, Nachtfaltern,
Spinnen, Fledermäusen.
Fremdling! Dein verlorner Schatten
Im Abendrot,
Ein finsterer Korsar
Im salzigen Meer der Trübsal.
Aufflattern weiße Vögel am Nachtsaum
Über stürzenden Städten
Von Stahl.

That in mad melancholy
A man would listen rapt.
O! you brazen times
Buried there in the sunset.

From the dark hallway stepped
The golden form
Of the young girl
Encircled by pale moons,
Autumnal retinue,
Snapped off black fir trees
In the night-storm,
The steep fortress.
O heart
Gleaming afar in snowy chill.

SLEEP

Second version

Confound you dark poisons,
White sleep!
This strangest of gardens
Twilit trees
Filled with snakes, night moths,
Spiders, bats.
Stranger! Your lost shadow
At sunset,
A gloomy corsair
In the salty sea of dolour.
White birds flutter up at night's border
Above crumbling cities
Of steel.

Ihr wilden Gebirge, der Adler
Erhabene Trauer.
Goldnes Gewölk
Raucht über steinerner Öde.
Geduldige Stille odmen die Föhren,
Die schwarzen Lämmer am Abgrund,
Wo plötzlich die Bläue
Seltsam verstummt,
Das sanfte Summen der Hummeln.
O grüne Blume –
O Schweigen.

Traumhaft erschüttern des Wildbachs
Dunkle Geister das Herz,
Finsternis,
Die über die Schluchten hereinbricht!
Weiße Stimmen
Irrend durch schaurige Vorhöfe,
Zerrißne Terrassen,
Der Väter gewaltiger Groll, die Klage
Der Mütter,
Des Knaben goldener Kriegsschrei
Und Ungebornes
Seufzend aus blinden Augen.

O Schmerz, du flammendes Anschaun
Der großen Seele!
Schon zuckt im schwarzen Gewühl
Der Rosse und Wagen
Ein rosenschauriger Blitz
In die tönende Fichte.
Magnetische Kühle
Umschwebt dies stolze Haupt,
Glühende Schwermut
Eines zürnenden Gottes.

Angst, du giftige Schlange,
Schwarze, stirb im Gestein!

You wild mountains, the eagles'
Exalted sorrow.
Golden cloud-forms
Smoky above stony wasteland.
Patient silence is breathed by the firs,
The black lambs by the abyss,
Where blueness suddenly
Grows strangely silent,
The gentle humming of bumble-bees.
O green flower –
O silence.

Dreamlike dark spirits
Of mountain torrent shake the heart,
Darkness
That breaks in upon chasms!
White voices
Wandering through eerie forecourts,
Shattered terraces,
The fearful wrath of fathers, the lament
Of mothers.
The young boy's golden war-cry
And the unborn life
Sighing out of blind eyes.

O pain, you flaming vision
Of a soul's greatness!
Now flashes in the black skirmish
Of horses and carts
Rose-quivering lightning
Into the resounding fir.
Magnetic coolness
Weaves about this proud head,
Glowing melancholy
Of a wrathful god.

Fear, you black venomous snake,
Die among rocks!

Da stürzen der Tränen
Wilde Ströme herab,
Sturm-Erbarmen,
Hallen in drohenden Donnern
Die schneeigen Gipfel rings.
Feuer
Läutert zerrissene Nacht.

DER ABEND

Mit toten Heldengestalten
Erfüllst du Mond
Die schweigenden Wälder,
Sichelmond –
Mit der sanften Umarmung
Der Liebenden,
Den Schatten berühmter Zeiten
Die modernden Felsen rings;
So bläulich erstrahlt es
Gegen die Stadt hin,
Wo kalt und böse
Ein verwesend Geschlecht wohnt,
Der weißen Enkel
Dunkle Zukunft bereitet.
Ihr mondverschlungnen Schatten
Aufseufzend im leeren Kristall
Des Bergsees.

DIE NACHT

Dich sing ich wilde Zerklüftung,
Im Nachtsturm
Aufgetürmtes Gebirge;
Ihr grauen Türme
Überfließend von höllischen Fratzen,
Feurigem Getier,

Then the wild torment
Of tears burst out,
Tempest-compassion,
The snowy summits around
Answer in threatening thunder.
Fire
Purifies shattered night.

EVENING

With dead heroes' forms
You, moon, fill
The mute forests,
Sickle-moon –
With the gentle embrace
Of lovers,
With shades of illustrious times
The mouldering rocks around;
So bluish it gleams forth
Towards the city
Where cold and evil
A decaying race dwells,
That shapes a dark future
For its white grandsons.
You moon-entwined shadows
Heaving sighs in empty crystal
Of the mountain lake.

NIGHT

You I sing wild craggy chasms
In tempest night
Towering mountains;
You grey towers
Brimming with hellish grimaces,
Fiery beasts,

Rauhen Farnen, Fichten,
Kristallnen Blumen.
Unendliche Qual,
Daß du Gott erjagtest
Sanfter Geist,
Aufseufzend im Wassersturz,
In wogenden Föhren.

Golden lodern die Feuer
Der Völker rings.
Über schwärzliche Klippen
Stürzt todestrunken
Die erglühende Windsbraut,
Die blaue Woge
Des Gletschers
Und es dröhnt
Gewaltig die Glocke im Tal:
Flammen, Flüche
Und die dunklen
Spiele der Wollust,
Stürmt den Himmel
Ein versteinertes Haupt.

DIE SCHWERMUT

Gewaltig bist du dunkler Mund
Im Innern, aus Herbstgewölk
Geformte Gestalt,
Goldner Abendstille;
Ein grünlich dämmernder Bergstrom
In zerbrochner Föhren
Schattenbezirk;
Ein Dorf,
Das fromm in braunen Bildern abstirbt.

Da springen die schwarzen Pferde
Auf nebliger Weide.
Ihr Soldaten!

Coarse ferns, firs,
Crystal flowers.
Unending torment,
That you hunted down God
Gentle spirit,
With deep sighs in cascading waters,
In swaying firs.

Golden flicker the fires
Of nations around.
Drunken with death
Over blackened cliffs
Plunges the fervid whirlwind.
The glacier's
Blue wave,
And the bell in the valley
Resounds with might:
Flames, curses
And the dark
Games of lustfulness,
Heaven is stormed
By a petrified head.

MELANCHOLY

Mighty are you dark mouth
Within, figure framed
From autumn cloud,
Golden silence of evening;
A greenish dusky mountain stream
In the shadowland
Of broken fir trees;
A village
That in brown images piously dies away.

There the black horses prance
Upon misty pastures.
You soldiers!

Vom Hügel, wo sterbend die Sonne rollt
Stürzt das lachende Blut –
Unter Eichen
Sprachlos! O grollende Schwermut
Des Heers; ein strahlender Helm
Sank klirrend von purpurner Stirne.

Herbstesnacht so kühle kommt,
Erglänzt mit Sternen
Über zerbrochenem Männergebein
Die stille Mönchin.

DIE HEIMKEHR

Zweite Fassung

Die Kühle dunkler Jahre,
Schmerz und Hoffnung
Bewahrt zyklopisch Gestein,
Menschenleeres Gebirge,
Des Herbstes goldner Odem,
Abendwolke –
Reinheit!

Anschaut aus blauen Augen
Kristallne Kindheit;
Unter dunklen Fichten
Liebe, Hoffnung,
Daß von feurigen Lidern
Tau ins starre Gras tropft –
Unaufhaltsam!

O! dort der goldene Steg
Zerbrechend im Schnee
Des Abgrunds!
Blaue Kühle
Odmet das nächtige Tal,
Glaube, Hoffnung!
Gegrüßt du einsamer Friedhof!

From the hill where the sun rolls dying
Gushes laughing blood –
Under oak trees
Speechless! O sullen melancholy
Of the host; a gleaming helmet
Fell ringing from scarlet brow.

Autumn night comes so coolly,
Shines forth with stars
Above men's splintered bones,
The silent sister-monk.

HOMEWARD JOURNEY

Second version

The coolness of dark years,
Pain and hope
Cyclopic cliffs preserve,
Mountains devoid of men,
The golden breath of autumn,
Evening cloud –
Purity!

Crystalline childhood
Gazes out of blue eyes;
Beneath dark fir trees
Love, hope,
That dew drips into rigid grass
From fiery eyelids –
Relentlessly!

O! the golden footbridge there
Breaking in the snow
Of the abyss!
Blue coolness
Is breathed by the night-dark valley,
Faith, hope!
Welcome you lonely graveyard!

Jüngling aus kristallnem Munde
Sank dein goldner Blick ins Tal;
Waldes Woge rot und fahl
In der schwarzen Abendstunde.
Abend schlägt so tiefe Wunde!

Angst! des Todes Traumbeschwerde,
Abgestorben Grab und gar
Schaut aus Baum und Wild das Jahr;
Kahles Feld und Ackererde.
Ruft der Hirt die bange Herde.

Schwester, deine blauen Brauen
Winken leise in der Nacht.
Orgel seufzt und Hölle lacht
Und es faßt das Herz ein Grauen;
Möchte Stern und Engel schauen.

Mutter muß ums Kindlein zagen;
Rot ertönt im Schacht das Erz,
Wollust, Tränen, steinern Schmerz,
Der Titanen dunkle Sagen.
Schwermut! einsam Adler klagen.

NACHTERGEBUNG

Fünfte Fassung

Mönchin! schließ mich in dein Dunkel,
Ihr Gebirge kühl und blau!
Niederblutet dunkler Tau;
Kreuz ragt steil im Sterngefunkel.

Purpurn brachen Mund und Lüge
In verfallner Kammer kühl;
Scheint noch Lachen, golden Spiel,
Einer Glocke letzte Züge.

Youth from that crystalline mouth
Sank your golden glance to vale;
Forest surge, all red and sere
In the black and evening hour.
Evening cuts so deep a wound!

Fear! Of Death the dream-oppressor,
All extinct the grave and year
Ready peers from tree and prey;
Fallow field and fertile earth.
Shepherd calls the fearful flock.

Sister, both your eyebrows blue
Beckon gently in the night.
Organ sighs and all Hell laughs
And the heart is terror-gripped;
Would on star and angel gaze.

Mother trembles for her babe;
Red resounds the ore in shaft,
Passion, tears and stony pain,
Shadowy legends of the Titans.
Melancholy! Eagles' lone lament.

SURRENDER TO NIGHT

Fifth version

Sister monk! Lock me in your darkness,
You mountains chill and blue!
Downbleeds dark dew;
Towers the Cross in starlight glitter.

Mouth and lying split in scarlet
In decrepit chamber chilling;
Seeming laughter, golden dalliance,
Of a bell the final ringing.

Mondeswolke! Schwärzlich fallen
Wilde Früchte nachts vom Baum
Und zum Grabe wird der Raum
Und zum Traum dies Erdenwallen.

IM OSTEN

Den wilden Orgeln des Wintersturms
Gleicht des Volkes finstrer Zorn,
Die purpurne Woge der Schlacht,
Entlaubter Sterne.

Mit zerbrochnen Brauen, silbernen Armen
Winkt sterbenden Soldaten die Nacht.
Im Schatten der herbstlichen Esche
Seufzen die Geister der Erschlagenen.

Dornige Wildnis umgürtet die Stadt.
Von blutenden Stufen jagt der Mond
Die erschrockenen Frauen.
Wilde Wölfe brachen durchs Tor.

KLAGE II

Schlaf und Tod, die düstern Adler
Umrauschen nachtlang dieses Haupt:
Des Menschen goldnes Bildnis
Verschlänge die eisige Woge
Der Ewigkeit. An schaurigen Riffen
Zerschellt der purpurne Leib
Und es klagt die dunkle Stimme
Über dem Meer.
Schwester stürmischer Schwermut
Sieh ein ängstlicher Kahn versinkt
Unter Sternen,
Dem schweigenden Antlitz der Nacht.

Moon cloud! Blackened tumble
Rampant fruits from trees at night,
And all space becomes a grave
And earth's pilgrimage a dream.

IN THE EAST

A people's gloomy wrath is like
Wild organs of a winter storm,
The scarlet wave of battle,
Of leaf-stripped stars.

With shattered brows, silver arms,
Night beckons dying soldiers.
In the shade of the autumn ash
The spirits of the vanquished sigh.

Thorny wilderness girds the city.
The moon hounds frightened women
From bleeding steps.
Wild wolves burst through the gate.

LAMENT II

Sleep and Death, the gloomy eagles,
Whirr all night about this head:
The icy wave of Eternity
May devour the golden image
Of Man. On horrid reefs
The crimson body is dashed
And the dark voice laments
Over the sea.
Sister of stormy melancholy,
Look, a tremulous boat is sinking
Beneath the stars,
To the mute countenance of Night.

GRODEK

Zweite Fassung

Am Abend tönen die herbstlichen Wälder
Von tödlichen Waffen, die goldnen Ebenen
Und blauen Seen, darüber die Sonne
Düstrer hinrollt, umfängt die Nacht
Sterbende Krieger, die wilde Klage
Ihrer zerbrochenen Münder.
Doch stille sammelt im Weidengrund
Rotes Gewölk, darin ein zürnender Gott wohnt
Das vergoßne Blut sich, mondne Kühle;
Alle Straßen münden in schwarze Verwesung.
Unter goldnem Gezweig der Nacht und Sternen
Es schwankt der Schwester Schatten durch den schweigenden Hain,
Zu grüßen die Geister der Helden, die blutenden Häupter;
Und leise tönen im Rohr die dunkeln Flöten des Herbstes.
O stolzere Trauer! ihr ehernen Altäre
Die heiße Flamme des Geistes nährt heute ein gewaltiger Schmerz,
Die ungebornen Enkel.

OFFENBARUNG UND UNTERGANG

Seltsam sind die nächtigen Pfade des Menschen. Da ich nachtwandelnd an steinernen Zimmern hinging und es brannte in jedem ein stilles Lämpchen, ein kupferner Leuchter, und da ich frierend aufs Lager hinsank, stand zu Häupten wieder der schwarze Schatten der Fremdlingin und schweigend verbarg ich das Antlitz in den langsamen Händen. Auch war am Fenster blau die Hyazinthe aufgeblüht und es trat auf die purpurne Lippe des Odmenden das alte Gebet, sanken von den Lidern kristallne Tränen geweint um die bittere Welt. In dieser Stunde war ich im Tod meines Vaters der weiße Sohn. In blauen Schauern kam vom Hügel der Nachtwind, die dunkle Klage der Mutter, hinsterbend wieder und ich sah die schwarze Hölle in meinem Herzen; Minute schimmernder Stille. Leise trat aus kalkiger Mauer ein unsägliches Antlitz – ein sterbender Jüngling – die Schönheit eines heimkehrenden Geschlechts. Mondesweiß umfing die Kühle des Steins die wachende Schläfe, verklangen die Schritte der Schatten auf verfallenen Stufen, ein rosiger Reigen im Gärtchen.

GRODEK

Second version

At evening the autumn woods resound
With deadly weapons, the golden plains
And blue lakes, the sun overhead
Rolls more darkly on; night embraces
Dying warriors, the wild lament
Of their broken mouths.
Yet silently red clouds, in which a wrathful god lives,
Gather on willow-ground
The blood that was shed, moon-coolness;
All roads flow into black decay.
Under the golden boughs of night and stars
Sister's shadow sways through the silent grove,
To greet the spirits of the heroes, the bleeding heads;
And softly the dark pipes of autumn sound in the reeds.
O prouder sorrow! You brazen altars,
The spirit's ardent flame today is fed by mighty grief,
The unborn generations.

REVELATION AND PERDITION

Strange are the night-paths of Man. While walking in sleep I wandered past stone rooms and a little lamp burned in each, a copper candlestick, and when I, sensing the chill, sank back upon the bed, there stood again at its head the black shadow of the woman-stranger and I buried my countenance in silence in these slow hands. The hyacinth also had flowered blue by the window and the ancient prayer sprang to the scarlet lips of the one who breathed, crystalline tears fell from his eyelids, wept for the bitter world. At that hour I was in my father's death the white son. The night wind blew from the hill in blue showers, Mother's dark lament dying away once more, and I saw black Hell within my heart; minute of shimmering silence. Silent an unutterable countenance emerged from a chalky wall – a dying youth – the beauty of a homing generation. Moon-white the coolness of stone embraced the waking brow, the footsteps of the shadows died upon derelict steps, a roseate round-dance in the little garden.

Schweigend saß ich in verlassener Schenke unter verrauchtem Holzgebälk und einsam beim Wein; ein strahlender Leichnam über ein Dunkles geneigt und es lag ein totes Lamm zu meinen Füßen. Aus verwesender Bläue trat die bleiche Gestalt der Schwester und also sprach ihr blutender Mund: Stich schwarzer Dorn. Ach noch tönen von wilden Gewittern die silbernen Arme mir. Fließe Blut von den mondenen Füßen, blühend auf nächtigen Pfaden, darüber schreiend die Ratte huscht. Aufflackert ihr Sterne in meinen gewölbten Brauen; und es läutet leise das Herz in der Nacht. Einbrach ein roter Schatten mit flammendem Schwert in das Haus, floh mit schneeiger Stirne. O bitterer Tod.

Und es sprach eine dunkle Stimme aus mir: Meinem Rappen brach ich im nächtigen Wald das Genick, da aus seinen purpurnen Augen der Wahnsinn sprang; die Schatten der Ulmen fielen auf mich, das blaue Lachen des Quells und die schwarze Kühle der Nacht, da ich ein wilder Jäger aufjagte ein schneeiges Wild; in steinerner Hölle mein Antlitz erstarb.

Und schimmernd fiel ein Tropfen Blutes in des Einsamen Wein; und da ich davon trank, schmeckte er bitterer als Mohn; und eine schwärzliche Wolke umhüllte mein Haupt, die kristallenen Tränen verdammter Engel; und leise rann aus silberner Wunde der Schwester das Blut und fiel ein feuriger Regen auf mich.

Am Saum des Waldes will ich ein Schweigendes gehn, dem aus sprachlosen Händen die härene Sonne sank; ein Fremdling am Abendhügel, der weinend aufhebt die Lider über die steinerne Stadt; ein Wild, das stille steht im Frieden des alten Hollunders; o ruhlos lauscht das dämmernde Haupt, oder es folgen die zögernden Schritte der blauen Wolke am Hügel, ernsten Gestirnen auch. Zur Seite geleitet stille die grüne Saat, begleitet auf moosigen Waldespfaden scheu das Reh. Es haben die Hütten der Dörfler sich stumm verschlossen und es ängstigt in schwarzer Windesstille die blaue Klage des Wildbachs.

Aber da ich den Felsenpfad hinabstieg, ergriff mich der Wahnsinn und ich schrie laut in der Nacht; und da ich mit silbernen Fingern mich über die schweigenden Wasser bog, sah ich daß mich mein Antlitz verlassen. Und die weiße Stimme sprach zu mir: Töte dich! Seufzend erhob sich eines Knaben Schatten in mir und sah mich strahlend aus kristallnen Augen an, daß ich weinend unter den Bäumen hinsank, dem gewaltigen Sternengewölbe.

Friedlose Wanderschaft durch wildes Gestein ferne den Abendweilern, heimkehrenden Herden; ferne weidet die sinkende Sonne auf kristallner Wiese und es erschüttert ihr wilder Gesang, der einsame Schrei des Vogels,

In silence I sat in a deserted inn under smoke-stained beams and alone with my wine; a radiant body inclined over a dark being and a dead lamb lay at my feet. Sister's pallid form emerged from putrifying blueness and so spoke her bleeding mouth: pierce black thorn. Oh my silver arms still resound with wild storms. Flow blood, from my moon-born feet, blossoming on night-dark paths over which the rat slips screaming. Flicker into life, you stars in my arched brows; and the heart rings softly in the night. A red shadow burst into the house with flaming sword, fled with snowy brow. O bitter death.

And a dark voice spoke from within me: I broke my black horse's neck in the midnight forest, when madness darted from his scarlet eyes; the shadows of the elms fell upon me, the blue laughter of the spring and the black coolnness of night, when I a wild huntsman put up a snowy quarry; in stony Hell my countenance expired.

And shimmering, a drop of blood fell into the lonesome man's wine; and as I drank from it, it tasted bitterer than the poppy; and a blackish cloud enveloped my head, the crystalline tears of angels that are damned; and softly did my sister's blood flow from its silver wound and fiery rain fell upon me.

By the forest edge will I walk, a silent being, for whom the harsh sun sank from speechless hands; a stranger by the evening hill who weeping lifts up his eyelids over the stony city; a wild creature that stands still in the peace of the ancient elder tree; o, unresting the twilit head listens, or hesitant steps follow the blue cloud by the hill, the grave stars also. Alongside the green shoots quietly give attendance, on mossy forest path the timid deer keeps one company. The huts of the villagers have closed mutely and the blue lament of the mountain stream in the black breathless calm is alarming.

But as I descended the rocky path madness seized me and I cried aloud in the night; and as I bent over the silent waters with silver fingers, I saw that my countenance had deserted me. And the white voice spoke to me: Kill yourself! Sighing there arose in me a young boy's shadow and gazed at me radiantly from crystalline eyes, that I sank down weeping beneath the trees, the mighty canopy of stars.

Relentless wandering through wild cliffs far removed from the evening hamlets, homing herds; far away the setting sun feasts on a crystalline meadow and her wild song is shattering, the solitary cry of a bird dying in blueness of peace. But silently you approach by night as I lay awake by the hill, or raging in springtime storms; and ever blacker does melancholy cloud

ersterbend in blauer Ruh. Aber leise kommst du in der Nacht, da ich wachend am Hügel lag, oder rasend im Frühlingsgewitter; und schwärzer immer umwölkt die Schwermut das abgeschiedene Haupt, erschrecken schaurige Blitze die nächtige Seele, zerreißen deine Hände die atemlose Brust mir.

Da ich in den dämmernden Garten ging, und es war die schwarze Gestalt des Bösen von mir gewichen, umfing mich die hyazinthene Stille der Nacht; und ich fuhr auf gebogenem Kahn über den ruhenden Weiher und süßer Frieden rührte die versteinerte Stirne mir. Sprachlos lag ich unter den alten Weiden und es war der blaue Himmel hoch über mir und voll von Sternen; und da ich anschauend hinstarb, starben Angst und der Schmerzen tiefster in mir; und es hob sich der blaue Schatten des Knaben strahlend im Dunkel, sanfter Gesang; hob sich auf mondenen Flügeln über die grünenden Wipfel, kristallene Klippen das weiße Antlitz der Schwester.

Mit silbernen Sohlen stieg ich die dornigen Stufen hinab und ich trat ins kalkgetünchte Gemach. Stille brannte ein Leuchter darin und ich verbarg in purpurnen Linnen schweigend das Haupt; und es warf die Erde einen kindlichen Leichnam aus, ein mondenes Gebilde, das langsam aus meinem Schatten trat, mit zerbrochenen Armen steinerne Stürze hinabsank, flockiger Schnee.

the secluded head, fearful lightning flashes startle the night-dark soul, your hands tear open my breathless breast.

As I walked in twilit gardens and the black figure of Evil had departed from me, the hyacinth stillness of the night embraced me; and I drifted upon a curved boat across the placid pond and sweet peace touched my stony brow. Speechless I lay under the ancient willows and the blue sky was high above me and full of stars; and as in my gazing I died by degrees, fear and the deepest of pains died within me; and the blue shade of the boy arose radiant in the darkness, gentle singing; there arose on moon-borne wings above the fresh green tree tops, crystalline cliffs, Sister's white countenance.

On silver soles I descended the thorny steps and I entered the lime-washed chamber. A candlestick burned silently there, and in silence I buried my head in scarlet linen; and the earth gave up a childlike body, a moon-born shape that slowly emerged from my shadow, sank with broken arms down stony steeps, flaky snow.

ST.-PETERS-FRIEDHOF

Ringsum ist Felseneinsamkeit.
Des Todes bleiche Blumen schauern
Auf Gräbern, die im Dunkel trauern –
Doch diese Trauer hat kein Leid.

Der Himmel lächelt still herab
In diesen traumverschlossenen Garten,
Wo stille Pilger seiner warten.
Es wacht das Kreuz auf jedem Grab.

Die Kirche ragt wie ein Gebet
Vor einem Bilde ewiger Gnaden,
Manch Licht brennt unter den Arkaden,
Das stumm für arme Seelen fleht –

Indes die Bäume blüh'n zur Nacht,
Daß sich des Todes Antlitz hülle
In ihrer Schönheit schimmernde Fülle,
Die Tote tiefer träumen macht.

NACHTSEELE

Dritte Fassung

Schweigsam stieg vom schwarzen Wald ein blaues Wild
Die Seele nieder,
Da es Nacht war, über moosige Stufen ein schneeiger Quell.

Blut und Waffengetümmel vergangner Zeiten
Rauscht im Föhrengrund.
Der Mond scheint leise in verfallene Zimmer,

ST PETER'S CHURCHYARD

All round is stony solitude.
The pallid flowers of death do shudder
On graves that mourn within the gloom –
Yet all this mourning knows no pain.

The heavens smile serenely down
Into this dream-enfolded garden,
Where silent pilgrims ever tend it.
Upon each grave the Cross holds vigil.

The church rears up like to a prayer
Before a sign of grace eternal,
Some candles burn beneath the arches
And mutely plead for wretched souls –

Whilst trees are flourishing by night,
That Death may hide his countenance
Within their beauty's shimmering plenty,
Which makes the dead dream deeper still.

NIGHT SOUL

Third version

Silent from the black forest descended a blue prey,
The soul,
As it was night, over mossy steps a snowy spring.

Blood and tumult of arms in times past
Rolls through the place of firs.
Quiet the moon shines into ruined rooms.

Trunken von dunklen Giften, silberne Larve
Über den Schlummer der Hirten geneigt;
Haupt, das schweigend seine Sagen verlassen.

O, dann öffnet jener die langsamen Hände
Verwesend in purpurnem Schlaf
Und silbern erblühen die Blumen des Winters

Am Waldsaum, erstrahlen die finstern Wege
In die steinerne Stadt;
Öfter ruft aus schwarzer Schwermut das Käuzchen den Trunknen.

Drunk with dark poisons, silver mask
Bent over the slumber of shepherds;
Head, mutely deserted by its legends.

O, then he opens his slow hands
Decaying in scarlet sleep
And silver the flowers of winter break into bloom

At the forest edge, the gloomy paths
Into the stony city begin to glow;
Often the little owl calls the drunken from black melancholy.

KLAGELIED

Die Freundin, die mit grünen Blumen gaukelnd
Spielt in mondenen Gärten –
O! was glüht hinter Taxushecken!
Goldener Mund, der meine Lippen rührt,
Und sie erklingen wie die Sterne
Über dem Bache Kidron.
Aber die Sternennebel sinken über der Ebene,
Tänze wild und unsagbar.
O! meine Freundin dcinc Lippen
Granatapfellippen
Reifen an meinem kristallenen Muschelmund.
Schwer ruht auf uns
Das goldene Schweigen der Ebene.
Zum Himmel dampft das Blut
Der von Herodes
Gemordeten Kinder.

Ein Teppich, darein die leidende Landschaft verblaßt
Vielleicht Genezareth, im Sturm ein Nachen
Aus Wetterwolken stürzen goldene Sachen
Der Wahnsinn, der den sanften Menschen faßt.
Die alten Wasser gurgeln ein blaues Lachen.

Und manchmal öffnet sich ein dunkler Schacht.
Besessene spiegeln sich in kalten Metallen
Tropfen Blutes auf glühende Platten fallen
Und ein Antlitz zerfällt in schwarzer Nacht.
Fahnen, die in finstern Gewölben lallen.

SONG OF LAMENT

My loved one, dallying with green flowers
Is playing in moonlit gardens –
O! what gleams beyond yew hedges!
Golden mouth that touches my lips,
And they ring out like stars
Over the brook Kidron.
Yet the nebulae of stars sink low over the plain,
Wild unutterable dances.
O! my beloved your lips
Pomegranate lips
Ripen by my crystalline shell-mouth.
Heavily there rests upon us
The golden silence of the plain.
Heavenwards steams the blood
Of the children
Murdered by Herod.

A carpet wherein the suffering landscape pales,
Perhaps Gennesaret, a light craft in the storm,
From thunder-clouds things golden tumble,
Madness that grips the gentle man.
The ancient waters burble in blue laughter.

At times a gloomy shaft is opened.
All the possessed are mirrored in chill metals,
Blood-drops fall onto glowing plates
And a countenance crumbles in the black night.
Banners that mumble in gloomy caverns.

Andres erinnert an der Vögel Flug
Über dem Galgen der Krähen mystische Zeichen
In spitzen Gräsern versinken kupferne Schleichen
In Weihrauchkissen ein Lächeln verhurt und klug.

Charfreitagskinder blind an Zäunen stehen
Im Spiegel dunkler Gossen voll Verwesung
Der Sterbenden hinseufzende Genesung
Und Engel die durch weiße Augen gehen
Von Lidern düstert goldene Erlösung.

DELIRIUM

Der schwarze Schnee, der von den Dächern rinnt;
Ein roter Finger taucht in deine Stirne
Ins kahle Zimmer sinken blaue Firne,
Die Liebender erstorbene Spiegel sind.
In schwere Stücke bricht das Haupt und sinnt
Den Schatten nach im Spiegel blauer Firne,
Dem kalten Lächeln einer toten Dirne.
In Nelkendüften weint der Abendwind.

AM RAND EINES ALTEN BRUNNENS

Zweite Fassung

Dunkle Deutung des Wassers: Zerbrochene Stirne im Munde der Nacht,
Seufzend in schwarzem Kissen des Knaben bläulicher Schatten,
Das Rauschen des Ahorns, Schritte im alten Park,
Kammerkonzerte, die auf einer Wendeltreppe verklingen,
Vielleicht ein Mond, der leise die Stufen hinaufsteigt.
Die sanften Stimmen der Nonnen in der verfallenen Kirche,
Ein blaues Tabernakel, das sich langsam auftut,
Sterne, die auf deine knöchernen Hände fallen,
Vielleicht ein Gang durch verlassene Zimmer,
Der blaue Ton der Flöte im Haselgebüsch – sehr leise.

Other things recall the flight of birds
Above the gallows, the crows' mystic signs,
In sharp grasses copper grass-snakes vanish,
In incense-pillows a smile grows wanton and sly.

Good Friday children sightless stand by fences
Mirrored in gloomy gutters filled with foulness,
The sickly sighs for health among the dying
And angels that through white eyes pass,
From eyelids darkly gleams golden salvation.

DELIRIUM

Black snow that dribbles from the roofs;
A blood-red finger dips into your brow,
Blue névés sink into the barren chamber,
That are the lifeless mirrors of lovers.
The head breaks into weighty pieces and ponders
On shadows mirrored in blue névés,
The frozen smile of a dead whore.
In sweet carnations weeps the evening breeze.

BY THE RIM OF AN ANCIENT WELL

Second version

Obscure reading of the waters: broken brow in the mouth of night,
Sighing in black pillow the boy's bluish shadow,
The sycamore's rustle, footsteps in the ancient park,
Chamber music dying on a winding stair,
Perhaps a moon which softly mounts the steps.
Nuns' gentle voices in the ruined church,
A blue tabernacle that slowly opens,
Stars that fall onto your skeletal hands,
Perhaps a stroll through deserted rooms,
The blue tone of the flute in the hazel bush – pianissimo.

Die Stille der Verstorbenen liebt den alten Garten,
Die Irre die in blauen Zimmern gewohnt,
Am Abend erscheint die stille Gestalt am Fenster

Sie aber ließ den vergilbten Vorhang herab –
Das Rinnen der Glasperlen erinnerte an unsere Kindheit,
Nachts fanden wir einen schwarzen Mond im Wald

In eines Spiegels Bläue tönt die sanfte Sonate
Lange Umarmungen
Gleitet ihr Lächeln über des Sterbenden Mund.

Die blaue Nacht ist sanft auf unsren Stirnen aufgegangen
Leise berühren sich unsre verwesten Hände
Süße Braut!

Bleich ward unser Antlitz, mondene Perlen
Verschmolzen in grünem Weihergrund.
Versteinerte schauen wir unsre Sterne.

O Schmerzliches! Schuldige wandeln im Garten
In wilder Umarmung die Schatten,
Daß in gewaltigem Zorn Baum und Tier über sie sank.

Sanfte Harmonien, da wir in kristallnen Wogen
Fahren durch die stille Nacht
Ein rosiger Engel aus den Gräbern der Liebenden tritt.

O das Wohnen in der Stille des dämmernden Gartens,
Da die Augen der Schwester sich rund und dunkel im Bruder aufgetan,
Der Purpur ihrer zerbrochenen Münder
In der Kühle des Abends hinschmolz.
Herzzerreißende Stunde.

The silence of the dead loves the ancient garden,
The madwoman who lived in blue rooms,
At evening the silent form appears at the window

Yet she let drop the yellowed curtain –
The trickle of glass beads recalled our childhood,
At night we found a black moon in the forest

Within a mirror's blueness the gentle sonata sounds
Long embraces
Her smile passes over the dying man's mouth.

The blue night has risen gently upon our brows.
Softly our putrid hands touch
Sweet bride!

Pale grew our countenance, moonlit pearls
Melted in the green pond's vale.
Turned to stone we gaze at our stars.

O painfulness! The guilty walk in the garden,
Shadows in wild embrace,
That tree and beast bore down on them in mighty wrath.

Gentle harmonies, as we in crystalline waves
Travel through the silent night
A rosy angel steps from the lovers' graves.

O our dwelling in the silence of the twilit garden,
When sister's eyes opened round and dark in her brother,
The scarlet of their broken mouths
Melted away in the coolness of evening.
Heart-rending hour.

September reifte die goldene Birne. Süße von Weihrauch
Und die Georgine brennt am alten Zaun
Sag! wo waren wir, da wir auf schwarzem Kahn
Im Abend vorüberzogen,

Darüberzog der Kranich. Die frierenden Arme
Hielten Schwarzes umschlungen, und innen rann Blut.
Und feuchtes Blau um unsre Schläfen. Arm' Kindlein.
Tief sinnt aus wissenden Augen ein dunkles Geschlecht.

AM ABEND

Ein blauer Bach, Pfad und Abend an verfallenen Hütten hin.
Hinter dunklen Gebüschen spielen Kinder mit blau und roten Kugeln;
Manche wechseln die Stirne und die Hände verwesen im braunen Laub.

In knöcherner Stille glänzt das Herz des Einsamen,
Schaukelt ein Kahn auf schwärzlichen Wassern.
Durch dunkles Gehölz flattert Haar und Lachen brauner Mägde.

Die Schatten der Alten kreuzen den Flug eines kleinen Vogels;
Geheimnis blauer Blumen auf ihren Schläfen.
Andere schwanken auf schwarzen Bänken im Abendwind.

Goldene Seufzer erlöschen leise in den kahlen Zweigen
Der Kastanie; ein Klang von dunklen Zymbeln des Sommers,
Wenn die Fremde auf der verfallenen Stiege erscheint.

AN NOVALIS

Erste Fassung

Ruhend in kristallner Erde, heiliger Fremdling
Vom dunklen Munde nahm ein Gott ihm die Klage,
Da er in seiner Blüte hinsank
Friedlich erstarb ihm das Saitenspiel
In der Brust,
Und es streute der Frühling seine Palmen vor ihn,
Da er mit zögernden Schritten
Schweigend das nächtige Haus verließ.

September the golden pear ripened. Sweetness of incense
And the dahlia burns by the old fence
Tell me! Where were we when on that black bark
Within evening we drifted by.

Above the crane flew on. Frozen arms
Held blackness in embrace, and within blood flowed.
And moist blueness about our brows. Poor little child.
With knowing eyes a dark race deeply muses.

AT EVENING

A blue brook, down path and evening past derelict huts.
Behind dark bushes children play with blue and red balls;
Some change their brow and hands decay in brown foliage.

In skeletal silence the heart of the lonely man gleams,
A bark sways upon blackish waters.
Through a dark coppice flutters the hair and laughter of brown maids.

Shadows of the aged cross the flight of a little bird;
Secret of blue flowers upon their temples.
Others reel on black benches in the evening breeze.

Golden sighs softly fade in the bare branches
Of the chestnut; a sound of dark summer cymbals,
When she the stranger appears on the derelict stair.

TO NOVALIS

First version

At rest in crystalline earth, sacred stranger,
A god took the lament from his dark mouth,
As in his flowering he sank low
The sound of strings died peacefully
Within his breast,
And Spring strewed its palms before him
As with faltering steps
He left the midnight house in silence.

AN NOVALIS

Zweite Fassung (a)

> In dunkler Erde ruht der heilige Fremdling.
> Es nahm von sanftem Munde ihm die Klage der Gott,
> Da er in seiner Blüte hinsank.
> Eine blaue Blume
> Fortlebt sein Lied im nächtlichen Haus der Schmerzen.

AN NOVALIS

Zweite Fassung (b)

> In dunkler Erde ruht der heilige Fremdling
> In zarter Knospe
> Wuchs dem Jüngling der göttliche Geist,
> Das trunkene Saitenspiel
> Und verstummte in rosiger Blüte.

STUNDE DES GRAMS

> Schwärzlich folgt im herbstlichen Garten der Schritt
> Dem glänzenden Mond,
> Sinkt an frierender Mauer die gewaltige Nacht.
> O, die dornige Stunde des Grams.
>
> Silbern flackert im dämmernden Zimmer der Leuchter des Einsamen,
> Hinsterbend, da jener ein Dunkles denkt
> Und das steinerne Haupt über Vergängliches neigt,
>
> Trunken von Wein und nächtigem Wohllaut.
> Immer folgt das Ohr
> Der sanften Klage der Amsel im Haselgebüsch.
>
> Dunkle Rosenkranzstunde. Wer bist du
> Einsame Flöte,
> Stirne, frierend über finstere Zeiten geneigt.

TO NOVALIS

Second version (a)

In dark earth the sacred stranger reposes.
From that gentle mouth the god took his lament
As in his flowering he sank low.
A blue flower
His song lives on in the midnight house of pain.

TO NOVALIS

Second version (b)

In dark earth the sacred stranger reposes
In tender bud
Within the youth the divine spirit grew,
Rapturous music of strings
And fell silent in rose-like flowering.

HOUR OF GRIEF

Footfall in black follows the gleaming moon
In the autumnal garden,
By freezing wall sinks the almighty night.
O, the thorny hour of grief.

Silver the solitary man's light flickers in twilit room,
Dying by degrees, since that man ponders a dark thing
And the stony head is bent over transience,

Drunk with wine and nocturnal harmony.
The ear ever follows
The thrush's gentle lament in the hazel bush.

Dark Rosary hour. Who are you
Solitary flute,
Forehead, freezing, bowed over gloomy times.

AN LUZIFER

Dritte Fassung

Dem Geist leih deine Flamme, glühende Schwermut;
Seufzend ragt das Haupt in die Mitternacht,
Am grünenden Frühlingshügel; wo vor Zeiten
Verblutet ein sanftes Lamm, der Schmerzen tiefsten
Erduldet; aber es folgt der Dunkle dem Schatten
Des Bösen, oder er hebt die feuchten Schwingen
Zur goldenen Scheibe der Sonne und es erschüttert
Ein Glockenton die schmerzzerrissene Brust ihm,
Wilde Hoffnung; die Finsternis flammenden Sturzes.

Rote Gesichter verschlang die Nacht,
An härener Mauer
Tastet ein kindlich Grippe im Schatten
Des Trunkenen, zerbrochenes Lachen
Im Wein, glühende Schwermut,
Geistesfolter - ein Stein verstummt
Die blaue Stimme des Engels
Im Ohr des Schläfers. Verfallenes Licht.

HEIMKEHR

Wenn goldne Ruh der Abend odmet
Wald und dunkle Wiese davor
Ein Schauendes ist der Mensch,
Ein Hirt, wohnend in der Herden dämmernder Stille,
Der Geduld der roten Buchen;
So klar da es Herbst geworden. Am Hügel
Lauscht der Einsame dem Flug der Vögel,
Dunkler Bedeutung und die Schatten der Toten
Haben sich ernster um ihn versammelt
Mit Schauern erfüllt ihn kühler Resedenduft
Die Hütten der Dörfler der Hollunder,
Wo vor Zeiten das Kind gewohnt.

TO LUCIFER

Third version

Unto this spirit lend your flame, glowing Melancholy;
Sighing the head rears up to midnight,
By fresh green springtime hill, where ages past
A gentle lamb once bled to death, endured
The deepest pain; and yet the man of darkness follows
The shade of Evil, or he uplifts his clammy wings
To the sun's golden disc and then a tolling bell
Shatters his pain-rent breast,
Wild hope; darkness in flaming fall.

Red faces devoured by Night,
Along the harsh wall
A childlike skeleton probes in the shade
Of the drunken man, broken laughter
In wine, glowing melancholy,
The spirit's torments – a stone grows mute
The angel's blue voice
In the ear of the sleeper. Derelict light.

HOMECOMING

When evening breathes golden repose
Forest and sombre meadow ahead
A contemplative being is Man,
A shepherd dwelling in the dusky silence of the herds,
The patience of the copper beeches;
So clear since autumn has come. By the hillside
The solitary man listens to the flight of birds,
To dark meaning and the shades of the dead
Have gathered more gravely about him;
The cool scent of resedas fill him with rapture,
The huts of villagers the elder-bush,
Where ages past the child lived.

Erinnerung, begrabene Hoffnung
Bewahrt dies braune Gebälk,
Darüber Georginen hangen,
Daß darnach er die Hände ringe
Im braunen Gärtchen den schimmernden Schritt
Verboten Lieben, dunkles Jahr,
Daß von blauen Lidern die Tränen stürzten
Dem Fremdling unaufhaltsam.

Von braunen Wipfeln tropft der Tau,
Da jener ein blaues Wild am Hügel erwacht,
Lauschend den lauten Rufen der Fischer
Am Abendweiher
Dem ungestalten Schrei der Fledermäuse;
Aber in goldener Stille
Wohnt das trunkene Herz
Seines erhabenen Todes voll.

TRÄUMEREI

Dritte Fassung

Verliebte gehn an den Hecken,
Die sich mit Düften füllen.
Am Abend kommen frohe Gäste
Von der dämmernden Straße.

Sinnige Kastanie im Wirtshausgarten.
Die feuchten Glocken sind verstummt.
Ein Bursche singt am Fluß
– Feuer, das Dunkeles sucht –

O blaue Stille! Geduld!
Wenn jegliches blüht.

Sanften Mut auch gib
Nacht dem Heimatlosen,
Unergründliches Dunkel
Goldne Stunde in Wein.

Remembrance, buried hope
These brown beams preserve,
Over which dahlias droop,
That for this he wrings his hands,
The shimmering stride in the little brown garden
Forbidden love, dark year,
That tears start from blue eyelids
Unrestrainable to the stranger.

Dew drips from brown tree-tops,
When that man awakens blue game by the hill,
Listening to the loud calls of the fishermen
By the evening pond
To the misshapen cry of bats;
Yet in golden silence
Dwells the enraptured heart
Replete with its sublime death.

REVERIE

Third version

Lovers pass along hedgerows
Which fill themselves with sweet scents.
At eventide glad guests arrive
From the twilit street.

Pensive chestnut tree in tavern garden.
The damp bells have grown silent.
A young lad sings by the stream
– Fire seeking out darkness –

O blue stillness! Patience!
When all things flower.

Gentle courage too give
Night to the homeless,
Unfathomable dark
Golden hour in wine.

Stille; als sänken Blinde an herbstlicher Mauer hin,
Lauschend mit morschen Schläfen dem Flug der Raben;
Goldne Stille des Herbstes, das Antlitz des Vaters in flackernder Sonne
Am Abend verfällt im Frieden brauner Eichen das alte Dorf,
Das rote Gehämmer der Schmiede, ein pochendes Herz.
Stille; in langsamen Händen verbirgt die hyazinthene Stirne die Magd
Unter flatternden Sonnenblumen. Angst und Schweigen
Brechender Augen erfüllt das dämmernde Zimmer, die zögernden Schritte
Der alten Frauen, die Flucht des purpurnen Munds, der langsam im Dunkel erlischt.

Schweigsamer Abend in Wein. Vom niedern Deckengebälk
Fiel ein nächtlicher Falter, Nymphe vergraben in bläulichen Schlaf.
Im Hof schlachtet der Knecht ein Lamm, der süße Geruch des Blutes
Umwölkt unsre Stirnen, die dunkle Kühle des Brunnens.
Nachtrauert die Schwermut sterbender Astern, goldne Stimmen im Wind.
Wenn es Nacht wird siehest du mich aus vermoderten Augen an,
In blauer Stille verfielen deine Wangen zu Staub.

So leise erlöscht ein Unkrautbrand, verstummt der schwarze Weiler im Grund
Als stiege das Kreuz den blauen Kalvarienhügel herab,
Würfe die schweigende Erde ihre Toten aus.

HERBSTLICHE HEIMKEHR

Dritte Fassung

Erinnerung, begrabene Hoffnung
Bewahrt dies braune Gebälk
Darüber Georginen hangen,
Immer stillere Heimkehr,
Der verfallne Garten dunklen Abglanz
Kindlicher Jahre,
Daß von blauen Lidern Tränen stürzen
Unaufhaltsam;
Hinüberschimmern der Schwermut
Kristallne Minuten
Zur Nacht.

Silence; as if the blind were sinking down by an autumn wall,
Listening with wasted brows for the flight of ravens;
Golden stillness of autumn, Father's countenance in flickering sunlight.
At evening the old village decays in the peace of brown oaks,
The red hammering of the forge, a beating heart.
Silence; in her slow hands the maid hides her hyacinth brow
Beneath fluttering sunflowers. Fear and silence
Of eyes breaking in death fills the twilit room, the wavering steps
Of the old women, the flight of the crimson mouth that slowly goes out in the gloom.

Muted evening in wine. From the low roof beams
Dropped a nocturnal moth, a nymph buried in bluish sleep.
In the yard the farmhand slaughters a lamb, the sweet smell of blood
Enclouds our brows, the dark coolness of the well.
The melancholy of dying asters lingers in sadness, golden voices in the wind.
When night comes you look upon me with mouldering eyes,
In blue stillness your cheeks turned to dust.

So silently a fire for weeds goes out, the black hamlet in the valley grows still
As if the Cross were to descend the blue hill of Calvary,
The mute earth to cast out its dead.

AUTUMN HOMECOMING

Third version

> Remembrance, these brown beams
> Preserve a buried hope
> Over which dahlias droop,
> Ever calmer homecoming,
> The derelict garden, dark reflection
> Of childhood years,
> That tears burst from blue eyelids
> Unceasingly;
> Crystalline minutes of melancholy
> Shimmer out
> Into the night.

NEIGE

Zweite Fassung

O geistlich Wiedersehn
In altem Herbst.
Gelbe Rosen
Entblättern am Gartenzaun,
Zu dunkler Träne
Schmolz ein großer Schmerz,
O Schwester!
So stille endet der goldne Tag.

LEBENSALTER

Geistiger leuchten die wilden
Rosen am Gartenzaun;
O stille Seele!

Im kühlen Weinlaub weidet
Die kristallne Sonne;
O heilige Reinheit!

Es reicht ein Greis mit edlen
Händen gereifte Früchte.
O Blick der Liebe!

DIE SONNENBLUMEN

Ihr goldenen Sonnenblumen,
Innig zum Sterben geneigt,
Ihr demutsvollen Schwestern
In solcher Stille
Endet Helians Jahr
Gebirgiger Kühle.

Da erbleicht von Küssen
Die trunkne Stirn ihm
Inmitten jener goldenen

DECLINE

Second version

O sacred reunion
In ageless autumn!
Yellow roses
Shed petals by the garden fence,
Mighty pain
Melted to a dark tear,
O Sister!
So silent ends this golden day.

SEASON OF LIFE

Purer in spirit the wild
Roses gleam by the garden fence;
O serene soul!

In cool vine-leaves
The crystalline sun feasts;
O sacred purity!

An aged man offers
Ripened fruit with noble hands.
O glance of love!

THE SUNFLOWERS

You golden sunflowers
Deeply inclined to death,
You lowly sisters
In such silence
Is Helian's year
Of mountain coolness ended.

Then his drunken brow
Grows pale with kisses
Amidst those golden

Blumen der Schwermut
Bestimmt den Geist
Die schweigende Finsternis.

So ernst o Sommerdämmerung.
Von müdem Munde
Sank dein goldner Odem ins Tal
Zu den Stätten der Hirten,
Versinkt im Laub.
Ein Geier hebt am Waldsaum
Das versteinerte Haupt –
Ein Adlerblick
Erstrahlt im grauen Gewölk
Die Nacht.

Wild erglühen
Die roten Rosen am Zaun
Erglühend stirbt
In grüner Woge Liebendes hin
Eine erblichene Rose

Flowers of melancholy
Silent darkness
Governs the spirit.

So grave o summer twilight.
From tired mouth
Your golden breath sank down the valley
To the abodes of shepherds,
Sinks beneath the leaves.
A vulture rears
His petrified head by the forest edge –
An eagle's glance
Ignites in the grey clouds
The night.

Wild glow
The red roses by the fence
In a green wave there dies away
A loving being aglow
A faded rose

DREAMLAND

An Episode

At times I must recall again those tranquil days which to me seem like a wondrous life lived happily, one I was able to enjoy unquestioningly, like a gift from unknown, beneficent hands. And that little town at the bottom of the valley is restored to my memory, with its broad main street extending through a long avenue of magnificent lime trees, with its crooked little side-streets filled with the secret and busy lives of petty tradesmen and artisans – and with its ancient town fountain at the centre of the square playing dreamily in the sunlight, and where at eventide the whisper of lovers blends with the murmur of the water. Yet the town seems to be dreaming of a bygone life.

And the gentle rolling contours of the hills, swept by solemn and silent pine forests, close off the valley from the world beyond. Their summits nestle gently against the distant, luminous heavens, and in this touching of earth and sky, the universe seems a part of one's native land. Human figures suddenly spring to mind and their past lives rise up before me with all their little sorrows and joys which these people felt free to confide in each other.

I lived eight weeks in this remoteness; those eight weeks seem to me like a detached and separate part of my life – a life apart – filled with an unutterable youthful joy, filled with a powerful yearning for distant beautiful things. It was here that my boyhood soul first received the impress of some great experience.

I see myself once more as a schoolboy in that little house with its little garden in front, situated some distance from the town and all but completely screened by trees and shrubbery. There I occupy a small attic room furnished with strange old, faded pictures. Here I dreamed away many an evening in silence, and the silence absorbed and preserved my heaven-bent, foolish and happy boyhood reveries and oftentimes brought them back to me once more in solitary twilight hours. In the evening I would often go down to my old uncle who spent almost the entire day with his ailing daughter Maria. We three would then sit together for hours in silence. The mellow evening breeze blew in at the window and wafted all manner of confused sounds to our ears, conjuring up for us vague dream-like images. And the air was filled with the strong scent of the roses which flowered by the garden fence. Slowly the night crept into our room and I would then rise, say

'Good night' and go up into my room, only to sit by the window for another hour, dreaming out into the night.

At first I felt something like an oppressed anxiety when I was near the little sick girl, which later changed into pious and reverential awe in face of this dumb and strangely moving suffering. Whenever I saw her, an obscure sensation would arise in me that she must surely die. And then I grew afraid to look her in the face.

Whenever I roamed the forests during the day, feeling so joyful in this solitude and peace, when I stretched out wearily on the moss and gazed for hours together into the bright, shimmering sky, into whose very depths one could see, when a strange and profound sense of joy thrilled me, I would suddenly think of the sick Maria – then I would get up and roam aimlessly about, overwhelmed by inexplicable thoughts and feel a dull pressure in my head and my heart which brought me to the verge of tears.

At times when I walked in the evening along the dusty main street which was filled with the scent of the blossoming lime and watched whispering couples as they stood in the shadows of the trees; when I saw two people pressed close together as though they were one being, sauntering slowly beside the fountain as it quietly played in the moolight, and a feverish thrill of presentiment coursed through me as I thought of poor sick Maria; then I was seized by a quiet yearning for something inexplicable and all at once I saw myself strolling arm in arm with her in the shade of the fragrant lime trees. And a strange radiance shone from Maria's great dark eyes, and the moon made her slender little face appear still paler and more transparent. Then I fled upstairs into my attic, leaned against the window, looked up into the deep dark heavens where the stars appeared to have gone out and for hours abandoned myself to formless and confusing dreams until overcome by sleep.

And yet – and yet I did not exchange so much as ten words with poor sick Maria. She never spoke. I would only sit at her side for hours gazing into her sick, suffering face, feeling ever and again that she must die.

In the garden I lay in the grass and breathed in the fragrance of a thousand flowers; my eye was intoxicated by the gleaming colours of blossoms flooded with sunlight, and I listened too for the silence in the air above, interrupted only by the mating call of a bird. I sensed the ferment of the fruitful, torrid earth, that mysterious sound of ever-creative life. I could then darkly feel the greatness and beauty of life. Then it semed to me as if life belonged to me. But then my eye lit upon the bay-window of the house. I could see the sick Maria sitting there – silent and motionless and with closed eyes. And all my thinking was again drawn to the suffering of this being and remained there –

became a painful but shyly conceded yearning which struck me as puzzling and confusing. And I left the garden timidly, silently, as though I had no right to linger in this temple.

Whenever I passed along that fence I would, half lost in thought, break off one of those big, glowing red roses that were heavy with scent. I then wanted to slip noiselessly past the window, when I glimpsed the delicate, trembling shadow of Maria's form contoured against the gravel path. And my shadow touched hers as though in an embrace. Then, as if taken with a fleeting thought, I stepped over to the window and laid the rose I had just broken off in Maria's lap. I then slid silently away, as though I feared being caught in the act. How often was this little course of events, which seemed so significant to me, repeated! I scarcely know. To me it is as if I had laid a thousand roses in the ailing Maria's lap, as if our shadows had embraced innumerable times. Never once did Maria mention this episode; yet from the gleam in her great radiant eyes, I sensed that she was happy about it.

Perhaps these hours, when we two sat together and in silence enjoyed a great, tranquil, deep joy, were so beautiful that I felt no need for any that were more beautiful still. My old uncle quietly left us to ourselves. One day, however, as I sat by him amongst all the resplendent flowers over which great golden butterflies hovered dreamily, he spoke to me in a quiet, thoughtful voice: 'Your soul is drawn to suffering, my boy.' And therewith he laid his hand upon my head as though wishing to add something more. Yet he remained silent. Perhaps he didn't know either what he had awakened in me by this, and what was mightily stirred to life in me from that day.

One day, as I again stepped over to the window where Maria sat as usual, I saw that her face had turned pale and rigid in death. Sunbeams darted across her bright, delicate form; her untied golden hair fluttered in the wind and it seemed to me as if no illness had carried her off but that she had died without visible cause – an enigma. I placed the last rose in her hand. She took it with her to the grave.

Soon after Maria's death I left for the city. But the memory of those tranquil days filled with sunshine have remained alive in me, more alive perhaps than the noisome present. I shall never again see the little town at the bottom of the valley – yes, I am loath to return to it again. I believe I should be unable to do so, even though I am at times seized by a deep yearning for those ever youthful things of the past. For I know that I should only look in vain for that which is lost without trace; I would no longer find there what lives on in my memory alone – just like the here and now – and what would that bring me but endless torment.

BARABBAS

A Fantasy

It happened then at the selfsame hour, as they led out the Son of Man towards Golgotha; that being the place where they take robbers and murderers to be executed.

It happened at the selfsame great and glowing hour, as his work was being accomplished.

It happened that, at the selfsame hour, a great throng of people was passing through the streets of Jerusalem with clamour – and right in the midst of the people strode Barabbas the murderer, and he carried his head high in defiance.

And about him were prostitutes in their finery, their lips painted red and their faces made up, and they snatched at him. And about him were men whose eyes wore a drunken look from wine and vices. But in all their speech lurked the sin of their flesh, and in the corruptness of their gestures lay the expression of their thoughts.

Many of those who met the drunken procession joined it and cried: 'Long live Barabbas!' And they all cried: 'Let Barabbas live!' Someone had also called out 'Hosannah!' The other one, however, they beat – for only a few days past they had cried out 'Hosannah!' to One who had entered the town as a king, and had strewn fresh palm branches in his path. But today they strewed red roses and shouted jubilantly: 'Barabbas!'

And as they went past a palace, they could hear the playing of strings and laughter and the noise of great festivities. And out of this house stepped a young man in festive clothing. And his hair gleamed with fragrant oils and his body was scented with the most precious unctions of Arabia. His eye beamed from the joys of feasting and the smile upon his mouth was lustful from the kisses of his lover.

When the youth recognized Barabbas, he stepped forward and spoke in this manner:

'Enter into my house, O Barabbas, and you shall recline upon my softest cushions; enter, O Barabbas, and my maidservants shall anoint your body with the most precious spikenard. At your feet a girl shall play her sweetest melodies upon the lute and from my most precious cup will I serve you my most ardent wine. And into this wine will I cast the most marvellous of my pearls. O Barabbas, be my guest for today – and my lover shall belong to my guest for this day, she who is lovelier than the dawn in springtime. Enter, O Barabbas, and wreathe your head with roses, rejoice in this day when he must die whose head they have crowned with thorns.'

And after the youth had thus spoken, the people shouted to him with joy and Barabbas rose up the marble steps like a victor. And the youth took the roses which wreathed his head and laid them about the brow of Barabbas the murderer.

Then he entered into his house with him, whilst the people on the streets rejoiced.

Barabbas reclined upon soft cushions; maidservants anointed his body with the choicest spikenards and at his feet sounded the gentle string-playing of a girl, and upon his lap sat the youth's lover who was lovelier than the dawn in springtime.

Laughter resounded – and the guests grew intoxicated with unimagined pleasures, they who were all enemies and despisers of the Only One – Pharisees and vassals of the priests.

At a given hour the youth commanded silence and all clamour ceased.

Then the youth filled his golden cup with the choicest wine, and in this vessel the wine became like glowing blood. He threw a pearl into it and offered the cup to Barabbas. The youth, however, clasped a cup made of crystal and raised it to Barabbas:

'The Nazarene is dead! Long live Barabbas!'

And all who were in the room cried out in jubilation:

'The Nazarene is dead! Long live Barabbas!'

And the people in the streets shouted:

'The Nazarene is dead! Long live Barabbas!'

Suddenly the sun went out, the earth shook to its foundations and a mighty terror passed through the world. All creatures trembled.

At the selfsame hour, the work of salvation was accomplished!

Outside the gates of the city of Jerusalem. Evening is approaching.

AGATHON: It is time for us to return to the city. The sun has gone down and it is growing dark over the city. It has grown very quiet. – But why don't you answer, Marcellus; why are you staring so vacantly into the distance?

MARCELLUS: I was just thinking, how out there in the distance the sea is washing the shores of this country; I was thinking how beyond the sea, the eternal, godlike city of Rome rears up to the stars, where no day passes without a festival. And here am I, standing on foreign soil. But I forgot. Surely it is time for you to return to the city. It's growing dark. And when twilight comes, there's a young girl waiting by the gates of Agathon's town. Don't let her wait, Agathon, don't let her wait, your lover. I tell you, the women of this country are very strange; I know, they are full of riddles. Don't let her wait, your lover; you never can tell what may happen. In an instant something terrible can happen. You should never let the moment pass you by.

AGATHON: Why are you speaking to me like this?

MARCELLUS: I'm just thinking, if she's beautiful, your lover, then you should not let her wait. I tell you, a beautiful woman is something never to be explained. The beauty of a woman is a riddle. One can never see through her. One never knows what a beautiful woman may be, or what she is compelled to do. That's the point, Agathon! Oh, I tell you – I knew one. I knew one and saw things that I'll never fathom. No one could ever fathom them. We never can see to the bottom of events.

AGATHON: What did you see happen? I beg you, tell me about it!

MARCELLUS: Well, let's walk on then. Perhaps the hour has come for me to be able to talk without having to quake at my own words and thoughts. (They walk slowly along the path back to Jerusalem. Silence is all about them.)

MARCELLUS: It all happened one torrid summer night when something feverish was lurking in the air and the moon made the senses reel. I saw her then. It was in a little tavern. She danced there, danced barefoot on a precious carpet. Never have I seen a woman dance more beautifully, more intoxicatingly; the rhythm of her body produced in me strange, dark dream-images, so that hot fevered thrills shook my body. It seemed to me as if this woman played in her dance with unseen, precious, secret things, as if she embraced godlike beings which no one saw, as if she kissed red lips which bent longingly to meet hers; her movements were the highest ecstasy; it seemed as if she were overpowered by caresses. She seemed to see things we did not see and she played with them in her dance, relished them in the incredible raptures of her body. Maybe she was raising her mouth to choice, sweet fruits and sipping a glowing wine as she tossed back her head and her gaze reached yearningly upwards. No! I could not grasp it, and yet all this was strangely alive – there it was. And then she sank down at our feet, unclothed, enveloped only by her hair. It was as if the night had gathered itself into her hair and now hid her from us. Yet she gave herself up, gave up her marvellous body, gave it up to anyone who wanted it. I saw her love beggars and common folk, princes and kings. She was the most magnificent hetaera. Her body was a precious vessel of pleasure; the world never saw a lovelier. Her life belonged to pleasure alone. I saw her dance at revels, when her body was showered with roses. Yet she stood in amongst the splendour of roses as a unique and lovely bloom which had just unfolded. I saw her wreathe the statue of Dionysus with flowers, saw her embrace the cold marble just as she embraced her lovers, choking them with her burning, fevered kisses. — And then came a man who passed by without a word, without a gesture, and was clothed in a hair shirt, and he had dust on his feet. He passed by and looked at her – and was gone. Yet she followed Him with her glance, froze in her movement – and went, went and followed that strange prophet who had perhaps summoned her with His eyes; followed His call and sank down at His feet. She humbled herself before Him – and looked up to Him as to a god; served Him just like the men who were about Him served Him.

AGATHON: You have not yet come to the end. I feel that you still want to say something more.

MARCELLUS: I don't know any more. No! But one day I heard that they wanted to nail that strange prophet to the cross. I heard it from our Governor Pilate. And then I wanted to go out to Golgotha. I wanted to see Him, to see Him die. Perhaps a mysterious event would then have been made clear to me. I wanted to look into His eyes; His eyes might possibly have spoken to me. I believe they would have spoken.

AGATHON: And still you didn't go!

MARCELLUS: I was on my way there. But I turned back. For I felt I would meet those others out there, on their knees before the cross, praying to Him, waiting for His last fleeting breath. In ecstasy. And so I turned back again. And things remained dark in my mind.

AGATHON: But that strange Man? – No, let's not talk about it!

MARCELLUS: Let's keep silent on that score, Agathon! We can do nothing else. – But look, Agathon, what strange dark light is glowing amongst the clouds. You would think a sea of flame is blazing behind the clouds. A divine fire! And the sky is like a blue bell. It's as if one can hear it tolling in deep, solemn tones. You might even suspect that up there above us, in unattainable heights, something is taking place of which we shall never know. But at times we can sense it, when that vast silence has settled over the earth. And yet! All this is very confusing. The gods have to pose insoluble riddles for us humans. And the earth does not rescue us from the cunning of the gods; for it too is full of things that confound the senses. Both things and humans confuse me. True enough! Things are very taciturn! And the human soul won't yield up its riddles. You ask and it keeps silent.

AGATHON: Let's live and not ask questions. Life is full of beauty,

MARCELLUS: There is much that we shall never know. Yes! And that's why it might be welcome to forget what we do know. Enough of that! We've almost reached our goal. Look how deserted our streets are. You can no longer see a soul. (A gust of wind rises.) That's a voice telling us that we should look up at the stars. And stay silent.

AGATHON: Look, Marcellus, how high the corn stands in the fields. Each stalk is bowed to the earth – laden with its fruit. There will be glorious days of harvesting.

MARCELLUS: Yes! Festive days! Days of feasting, Agathon my friend!

AGATHON: I shall walk through the fields with Rachel, through the fruit-laden, blessed fields! O joy of life!

MARCELLUS: You are right! Rejoice in your youth. Youth is beauty. It befits me to walk in the dark. But here our paths divide. You are expected by your lover – I, by the silence of the night. Farewell Agathon! It will be a glorious and beautiful night. One can stay out in the open for a long while.

AGATHON: And can gaze up at the stars – towards the great calm. I shall go joyfully on my way and sing the praises of beauty. That is how one does honour to oneself and the gods.

MARCELLUS: Do as you say and you will do right! Farewell, Agathon!

AGATHON (thoughtfully): I only wish to ask one more thing of you. Think nothing of my asking this. What was the name of that strange prophet? Tell me!

MARCELLUS: What use is it to you to know that! I've forgotten his name. But no! I remember. I remember. His name was Jesus and he was from Nazareth.

AGATHON: I thank you! Farewell! May the gods smile on you, Marcellus! (He leaves.)

MARCELLUS (lost in thought): Jesus! – Jesus! And he was from Nazareth. (He goes on his way slowly and thoughtfully. Night has fallen and in the sky countless stars are shining.)

DESOLATION

1

Nothing more can break the silence of desolation. Above the sombre, ancient tree-tops the clouds float by mirrored in the greenish-blue waters of the lake which appears bottomless. And motionless, as though plunged into mournful resignation, the tranquil surface reposes – day in, day out.

At the centre of the silent lake, a castle rears up to the clouds with its sharp, ragged towers and roofs. Weeds tumble over the black, broken walls and sunlight rebounds from the round, clouded windows. Doves fly about in the gloomy, dark courtyards and seek shelter in the crevices of walls.

They seem to fear something, for they fly in shy haste past the windows. Below in the courtyard a fountain plashes with a dim light sound. Now and then the thirsting doves drink from a bronze fountain basin.

Through the narrow, dusty alleyways of the castle a stifling, feverish breath is wafted, making the bats flutter up in fright. Nothing else disturbs the deep silence.

Yet the great rooms are all black with dust! High, bare and frosty, and filled with derelict objects. At times a tiny gleam pierces the clouded windows and once more the darkness swallows it up. Here the past has died.

Here it has petrified at some moment into a single, distorted rose. Heedlessly time passes its insubstantiality by.

And the silence of desolation permeates everything.

2

No one may force their way into the park any more. The branches of the trees are locked in a thousandfold embrace; the whole park is nothing but a single gigantic living being.

And everlasting night weighs heavily beneath the giant canopy of leaves. And deepest silence! And the air is saturated with the musty vapours of decay!

Yet sometimes the park is roused from its troubled dreams. It then exudes recollections of starlit nights, of deep hidden secret places, where it spied on fevered kisses and embraces, of summer nights filled with ardent splendour and glory, when the moon conjured up confused images upon the black background, of people who walked beneath its leafy canopy with gentle grace, replete with rhythmic motion, people who exchanged sweet, mad, murmured words and subtle alluring smiles.

And then the park sinks back once more into its death-like slumber.

Upon the waters the shadows of copper beeches and firs are swayed and a sad, muted murmur rises from the depths of the lake.

Swans glide across the gleaming waters, slowly stretching up their slender necks, motionless and stiff. On they glide! Around the defunct castle! Day in, day out!

Pallid lilies grow by the edge of the lake in amongst garish grasses. And the shadows they cast on the waters are paler than themselves.

And when these have died away, others come up from the deep. And they are like little, dead female hands.

Great curious fish swim about the pallid flowers with staring, glassy eyes and plunge once more into the deep – without a sound!

And the silence of desolation permeates everything.

3

High up there in the crumbling chamber of the tower sits the count. Day in, day out.

With his eyes he follows the clouds which float by over the tree-tops, resplendent and pure. He is glad to see the sun as it glows amongst the clouds at eventide when it is setting. He listens for every sound in the heights: for the cry of a bird that flies past the tower or for the resonant blast of the wind as it sweeps about the castle.

He sees how that park lies in its dull and heavy sleep, and watches the swans glide across the glittering waters as they swim about the castle. Day in, day out!

And the waters have a greenish-blue sheen. Yet in the waters the clouds are mirrored as they float above the castle, and the shadows they cast upon the waters have a pure and luminous gleam no less than their own. The water-lilies beckon to him like little dead female hands, and they sway in sad reverie to the quiet sounds of the wind.

The poor count looks down upon all that surrounds him there in death, like a little bewildered child threatened by some disaster; one who no longer has the strength to live, who pines away like the shades of the morning.

He listens only to the little, sad melody of his soul; vanished past!

When evening has come, he lights his old, blackened lamp and reads about bygone greatness and glory in massive, yellowing books.

He reads with a fevered, resonant heart until the present day, to which he does not belong, dies away. Then the shadows of the past rise up – giant-like. And he lives this life; the marvellous and lovely life of his forebears.

Some nights when the tempest hurtles about the tower, so that walls reverberate to their foundations and the birds scream in fright outside his windows, the count is overcome by an unspeakable sadness.

Disaster weighs upon his age-old, exhausted soul.

And he presses his face against the window and looks out into the night. Everything then appears to him gigantic and dreamlike, ghostly! And terrible. He hears the storm raging through the castle as though it wanted to sweep out all that is dead and gone and scatter it to the winds.

Yet when the confused image of night dies away like a shade summoned up – everything is once more permeated by the silence of desolation.

p. 3   'The Ravens' – probably written August 1909. *l.* 9 'keifen' (to scold, squabble) is unconventional when applied to birds (see also line 9 of 'The Rats', p. 17 below).

p. 3   'Amid Red Foliage Full of Guitars' – probably between July 1910 and February 1911. *l.* 14 'Verwesung' (decay) rhyming with 'Genesung' (restoration) is an early example of the tensions Trakl creates between associated polar opposites.

p. 5   'Music in the Mirabell' – the Mirabell Garden is a formal baroque pleasure garden in Salzburg (dating from 1700) set on the right river bank opposite the city centre. This terraced garden with its trim hedges and marble statues is one of the gems of the city.

p. 5   'Dusk in Winter' – *l.* 2 'Kreuz' may be read as 'cross' or 'across', though in the first case a noun would make little sense in grammatical terms. Max von Esterle, an artist also associated with the 'Brenner circle', portrayed Trakl and designed his exlibris.

p. 7   'The Beautiful City' – The city which is here evoked is the poet's birthplace Salzburg. The house in which he was born, Waagplatz 2, stands adjacent to the Kapitelplatz with its marble fountain.

p. 11   'Melancholy' – In the earlier versions of this poem Trakl wavers between the superscriptions 'Melancholy' and 'Melancholia'. All three versions were written in Salzburg between 20 February and 31 March 1913. *l.* 2 The phrase 'im Vorübergleiten' ('in gliding by') is ambivalent in its syntactical relations.

p. 11   'Transfigured Autumn' – Written in Salzburg, May 1912, the poem shows traces of the influence of the German Romantic poet Joseph, Freiherr von Eichendorff (1788–1857), though an individual style has clearly asserted itself already.

p. 13   'Forest Nook' – Karl Minnich (1886–1964), lawyer. A friend of the poet since school and university days. *l.* 4 The phrase 'gibt das Geleite' ('keeps company') has definite associations with death, i.e. 'das letzte Geleit geben' ('to pay one's last respects').

p. 15   'Mankind' – probably written in Innsbruck between 26 September and 10 October 1912. The imagery refers obliquely to Christ's agony in the garden and his betrayal. *l.* 5 'rotes Geld' suggests blood money, i.e. the forty pieces of silver paid to Judas Iscariot. There may also be a connection with Mephisto's words on 'rotes Gold' in Goethe's *Faust Part I*, *l.* 1679.

p. 15   'De Profundis' – written late 1912, probably in Innsbruck. The clear influence of Rimbaud ('Enfance') may be traced in the repetitions of the first three lines (cf. also 'Psalm I'), but also in vocabulary and illogically connected images. Trakl read Rimbaud in the translation by K. L. Ammer (Leipzig, 1907). The prominence of the 'I' in the latter half of the poem is noteworthy since Trakl assiduously avoided the first person as a rule.

p. 17   'Trumpets' – *l.* 1 'Weiden' (willows) symbolize grief or mourning (cf. also

'Grodek') and this meaning extends also to the sycamore and the grove. In *l.* 8 'Lachen' can mean 'laughter' as well as 'pools'.

p. 17 'Psalm I' – first published in *Der Brenner*, III, 1912/13. The influence of Rimbaud is again to be noted in the patterned repetitions, the free rhythms and the collage of imagery in which the pagan and Christian worlds are juxtaposed. The poem is, by contrast to 'De Profundis', distinctive for its suppression of the 'I' form. The absence of a divinity (*deus absconditus*) in the former is answered by the reference to 'God's golden eyes' in the final line of 'Psalm'.

p. 21 'Songs of the Rosary' – first published in *Der Brenner*, III, 1912/13. The poems were only later composed into a trilogy (cf. letter to E. Buschbeck late March 1913). *l.* 8 in 'Amen': 'Azrael's shadow' refers to the Angel of Death. He is mentioned also in Trakl's fragmentary puppet play *Blaubart* ('Bluebeard') (*l.* 189): 'hörst du des Asrael Flügelschlag' ('do you hear Azrael's wing-beat'). It is quite probable that Trakl's first encounter with this grim messenger of mortality came via Edgar A. Poe, in whose 'Ligeia' and 'Mesmeric Revelation' Azrael notably figures.

p. 23 'Decay' – An earlier version of this poem was written in Vienna in June or July 1909. It reveals the strong influence of the Austrian poet Lenau (pseudonym of Nikolaus Niembsch, Edler von Strehlenau, 1802–50) in respect of tone and vocabulary. A few telling changes show the poet reaching for his characteristic words: *l.* 5 'nachtverschlossen' ('night-enclosed') becomes 'dämmervollen' ('filled with twilight'), *l.* 10 'Ein Vogel' ('a bird') becomes 'Die Amsel' ('the blackbird'), *l.* 14 'fahle Astern' ('pale asters') becomes 'blaue Astern' ('blue asters').

p. 23 'In the Village' – first published in *Der Ruf*, no.4, Vienna and Leipzig, May 1913.

p. 27 'Evening Song' – first published in *Der Brenner*, III, 1912/13. *l.* 9 the verb 'schweigt' ('is silent') used with a genitive to indicate an object is unusually forceful.

p. 27 'Three Glances into an Opal' – Erhard Buschbeck (1889–1960) was a man of letters, literary editor of several journals, and artistic director of the Burgtheater in Vienna in his later years. Like Trakl, a baptised Lutheran, he was a close friend since his schooldays and helped him in placing his first published poems. He also edited the anthology of Trakl's early verse *Aus goldenem Kelch* (1939), first published in *Salzburg. Ein literarisches Sammelwerk*, Salzburg, January 1913. The fusion of images of the sacred and beautiful with those of the profane and ugly is derivative of the style of Baudelaire's *Les Fleurs du Mal*. *l.* 29 'Gauch' has a profusion of meanings; apart from 'cuckoo' it may signify a simpleton, dupe or cuckold.

p. 31 'Night Song' – first published in *Der Brenner*, III, 1912/13. The words 'Odem' ('breath') in *l.* 1 and 'Antlitz' ('countenance') in *l.* 5 are elevated poetic forms to which Trakl generally adheres. 'Elai' in *l.* 5 recalls Christ's words on the Cross (Matthew 27:46). The second version ends with the words 'Ich bin vollbracht' ('I am accomplished'), a clear reference to the final words on the Cross. *l.* 2 'ihrer Heiligkeit' ('of her sacredness') is not linked grammatically but could be read as dependent on 'erstarrt' ('stiffens').

p. 31 'Helian' – written in December 1912 and January 1913, it is Trakl's longest poem; 'the dearest and most painful I have ever written' as he wrote to Erhard Buschbeck. The title derives from the early Lower Saxon Gospel poem *Heliand* (ca. 830) meaning 'Heiland' ('Saviour') and is also connected with the name Helios, the Greek sun-god. The interaction of pagan and Christian myth is reminiscent of Hölderlin's late hymns, as is much in the tone and the diction. Rilke, who was profoundly impressed by the poem, wrote to Ludwig von Ficker in February 1915: 'it was for me most moving through its inner intervals; it is, as it were, built up upon its pauses, a few boundaries embracing what is infinitely wordless: that is how the lines stand.'

p. 39 From *Sebastian im Traum* (*Sebastian in a Dream*) – the title of the first major collection of Trakl's work published by Kurt Wolff, Leipzig 1915.

p. 39 'Song of Hours' – *l.* 2 'starrender' means 'grown rigid' as well as 'staring'; both senses might be adduced here. *l.* 4 'der Gesegneten' might be read as a genetive plural but a feminine singular is a more plausible rendering, especially since 'die Gesegnete' can mean 'the pregnant woman' as well as 'a woman blessed'. An earlier variant of the *l.* 5 reads 'Gebenedeit ist des Weibes Leib' ('blessed is the woman's body'), a phrase almost identical with the Angel Gabriel's address to Mary (Luke 1:28).

p. 43 'To the Boy Elis' – written April 1913 on the Hohenburg (Salzburg). The name 'Elis' recalls the figure created by Hugo von Hofmannsthal in his early play *Das Bergwerk zu Falun* (1899). Hofmannsthal had derived his subject from E. T. A. Hoffmann's tale *Die Bergwerke zu Falun* (1818) which tells of a young man, Elis Fröböm, lured to his death down a mine, whose corpse was perfectly preserved there and brought to the surface years later where it is recognized by his former love, now an old woman, and ardently embraced. Trakl weaves together his own imagery to create a more ethereal figure overshadowed by death.

p. 45 'Elis' – written in conjunction with the previous poem and based on the same figure. In the second version the two lyrics together formed a triadic poem.

p. 49 'Sebastian in a Dream' – The titular poem of the collection refers to the martyred saint whose effigy, transfixed by arrows, may often be seen flanking a baroque altar in an Austrian or South German church. Apart from being a patron saint of archers, huntsmen, soldiers and gunsmiths, he is also the patron of ironmongers (the trade of Trakl's father). His feast day is 20 January. The Church of St Sebastian with its cemetery stands on the right bank of the city of Salzburg in the Linzer Gasse. *l.* 15 'St Peter's autumn churchyard': the churchyard of that name with its catacombs nestles under the rock of the Mönchsberg in Salzburg. *l.* 27 'Kalvarienberg' ('Mount Calvary'); this name also attaches locally to part of the rocky hill approached by a steep and gloomy path skirted by stations of the cross which are represented in life-sized sculptures. *l.* 48 'Osterglocke' (means both 'daffodil' and 'Easter bell').

p. 55 'By the Mönchsberg' – one of the hills on the left bank of the river forming part of the city of Salzburg. The highest point (542 meters) is formed by the castle Hohen-salzburg. *l.* 2 'Hütten von Laub' seems a direct pointer to 'Laubhüttenfest' ('Feast of Tabernacles'), the ancient Jewish harvest thanksgiving in early October.

p. 55   'Kaspar Hauser Song' – The title recalls a foundling of that name who mysteriously appeared in Nürnberg in the year 1828 and whose origins remained unknown. Although a youth of about eighteen, he was innocent of language and of the world, a stranger to society and removed from the ways of men. He had apparently spent all his earlier life captive and hidden in a dismal cell. He drew the attention of many men of science, including that of the philosopher Ludwig Feuerbach. His legendary status was enhanced by a whole succession of poets and writers (among them Verlaine, Jakob Wassermann, Stefan George, Rilke and Peter Handke, and by Werner Herzog's film *The Enigma of Kaspar Hauser*, 1974). Trakl, who was especially drawn to this figure, once wrote to Buschbeck in 1912: 'Why all the agony. I shall after all for ever remain a Kaspar Hauser.' *l.* 10 'Ich will ein Reiter werden' ('I want to be a rider') is, almost verbatim, the sole coherent sentence the historical Kaspar Hauser had learnt from his gaoler.

p. 57   'Transformation of Evil' – written in Innsbruck between 16 September and 15 October 1913. This mysterious prose poem consists of a complex web of dreamlike imagery, in part reminiscent of Novalis's *Hymns to Night* (see note to pp. 143–5 below). The visionary quality is enhanced by the dislocated, unmediated linguistic forms which recalls the style of Rimbaud's *Les Illuminations*. The pronoun 'jener' in the penultimate sentence (literally 'that one' or 'that man') is an emphatic pointer to some significant person. It has been rendered as 'the One' to indicate the supreme importance of the unspecified person.

p. 65   'Sonja' – The name most probably refers to the figure in Dostoyevsky's novel *Crime and Punishment*. However, another impressive character named Sonja is the mother of the hero in the same author's *A Raw Youth*. Trakl was powerfully drawn to the Russian novelist and read him extensively. The moral–aesthetic tensions inherent in the prostitute Sonja's life, combining sinfulness with innocence, physical destitution and spiritual beauty, are hinted at through the imagery.

p. 67   'Autumn Soul' – *l.* 8 'stad' (one of Trakl's rare Austrian colloquialisms meaning 'quiet', 'calm', 'still').

p. 69   'Afra' – St Afra was burnt as a prostitute under the Emperor Diocletian (*c.* AD 304) and is honoured as the patroness of the diocese of Augsburg and of prostitutes. Trakl's choice of this colourful saint relates to his deep sense of individual sin and its corollary, the hope of redemption. The final line is a recognizable echo of the last line of Hölderlin's great poem 'Patmos': 'dem folgt deutscher Gesang' ('thereafter follows German song').

p. 71   'Peace and Silence' – *ll.* 11–12 – though written apart, the two lines form a single sentence in which an identity between 'youth' and 'sister' is established. The phrase 'black decay' figures again in 'Grodek'.

p. 71   'Anif' – the name of a rural village some 18 kilometers south of Salzburg.

p. 75   'Decline' – the genesis of this poem shows a complete transformation of the material through all five versions, so that the earlier ones in fact constitute individual poems. Only the two final lines remain as constants in versions three to five: the image of the 'Zeiger' ('hands of a clock', or 'pointers') being closely associated with the passage of time and with a clear function (indication), yet this is, typically for Trakl , counteracted by the qualifying term 'blind'.

p. 77 'Spiritual Twilight' – *l.* 1 'Stille' can be read either as a noun ('silence') or as an adverb. The first version ends quite differently with the lines:

> Aus schwarzem Verfall
>
> Treten Gottes strahlende Engel.
>
> Out of black decay
>
> Arise God's radiant angels.

p. 77 'Song of the Western World' – *l.* 21 The word 'Geschlecht' may be read as 'race', 'generation' or 'sex'. The last meaning suggests itself with most conviction in view of the surrounding imagery which points to a beatific, transfigured state for the lovers in which individuation ceases to be. The word 'ein' is emphasized as Trakl intended.

p. 81 'Föhn' – the name given to the warm wind that crosses the Alps from the South and which affects the climate north of the range. It is associated with all kinds of mood changes such as depression, irritability and headache but also more violent psychic reactions including suicide. *l.* 9 is reminiscent of a line in Hölderlin's 'Abendphantasie' ('Evening Fantasy'): 'Warum schläft denn nimmer nur mir in der Brust der Stachel?' ('Why then does the thorn in my breast alone never sleep?')

p. 83 'Karl Kraus' – Karl Kraus (1874–1936), Austrian satirist, critic and tireless crusader for ethical truth in the use of language, proved a congenial spirit for Trakl, whose own quest for pristine purity of expression made him a natural ally. Trakl also dedicated his earlier poem 'Psalm I' to Kraus (p. 17, above).

p. 83 'To Those Grown Silent' – *l.* 5 'versunkene' ('sunken') may also be read as 'engrossed'.

p. 83 'Passion' – the primary meaning of the title is religious; the references to Christ's Passion are explicit in the two earlier versions but have disappeared from the final one.

p. 85 'Sevenfold Song of Death' – *l.* 2 'Untergang' ('decline') refers equally to sunset and to the idea of waning. *l.* 10 'Erscheinender' is a mysterious adverbial form: it constitutes a novel comparative of 'appearing' and it echoes the use of the verb 'erscheint' in *l.* 4.

p. 89 'In Venice' – *l.* 8 The verb 'starrt' is here wholly ambivalent; it signifies both the idea of rigidity and of staring starkly. The image of the head of the Medusa is evidently invoked.

p. 93 'Song of a Captive Blackbird' – *l.* 1 Trakl uses the obsolete poetic word 'Odem' for 'breath' for its fuller spiritual associations as in the Book of Genesis 2:7: 'und er blies ihm ein den lebendigen Odem in seine Nase' ('and breathed into his nostrils the breath of life').

p. 95 'Summer's Decline' – The obscure concluding lines are introduced by the hortative 'Gedächte' ('If only it were mindful'). The term 'ein Wild' signifies a hunter's 'game' (a wild creature) or 'prey'.

p. 97 'The West' – Else Lasker-Schüler (1869–1945), pen name of Elisabeth Schüler, was primarily a lyric poet who also wrote prose fiction and plays. Her first collection of verse appeared in Berlin in 1902. Much admired by contemporary poets and painters alike, she led an eccentric, nomadic life in Germany and later in Palestine. She lies buried in the Jewish cemetery on the Mount of Olives. The longer second version in five parts was executed in late March 1914. The last line of part four reads 'Gewaltig schweigen die Mauern rings' ('with might the walls around are mute') which is close to some lines in Hölderlin's late poem 'Hälfte des Lebens' ('Half of Life').

p. 99 'Springtime of the Soul II' – *l.* 24 The word 'Geleit' puns on 'Geläut' ('tolling of bells') in the Austrian pronunciation. *l.* 25 Myrtle, traditionally signifying 'love', it was sacred to the goddess Aphrodite in antiquity and later associated with the bridal wreath in marriage. *l.* 26 'Lidern' ('eyelids') is phonetically identical with 'Liedern' ('songs'), a conflation of sound and sense reminiscent of the well-known lines from Hofmannsthal's poem 'Manche freilich':

> Ganz vergessener Völker Müdigkeiten
> Kann ich nicht abtun von meinen Lidern. . .
> The tiredness of peoples quite forgotten
> I cannot remove from my eyelids. . .

p. 103 'Song of the Recluse' – Karl Borromaeus Heinrich (1884–1938), contributor to and collaborator on *Der Brenner*. He was well regarded at the turn of the century as the author of several novels. *l.* 6 'dämmert' ('grows dark') is used with the dative in a strikingly original manner; the sense is of a spiritual state of encroaching gloom besetting Man's pensive brow. *l.* 7 'das Gute' ('goodness') is syntactically dislocated so that it relates both to subject and object of the sentence. *l.* 16 'der Duldende' ('one who suffers, endures') has connotations of bearing a burden in silence and so of the Christian idea of suffering.

p. 103 'Dream and Derangement' – the term 'Umnachtung' ('derangement, insanity') is far more evocative in German and suggests 'a darkening of the mind' or a 'nightfall of the mind', as it were. This deeply personal prose poem was probably written in Innsbruck at the beginning of the year 1914. In it are reflected numerous motifs and formulations from the poet's earlier work, but there are also definite echoes of Novalis and Hölderlin. *l.* 96 'Geäst des Stammes' ('branches of the stem') is at the same time a reference to lineage and descent (i.e. family tree) since the consciousness of forming part of a 'degenerate' and 'accursed' race runs like a red line through the poem.

p. 111 'In Hellbrunn' – written between 6 March and 15 May 1914. Schloss Hellbrunn is situated some 5 kilometers south of Salzburg. It was built as an archiepiscopal residence in the years 1613–19 in the early baroque style and is noted for its extensive pleasure gardens with fountains, grottos and statuary.

p. 111	'The Heart' – probably dating from between May and 1 July 1914. *l.* 25 'Jünglingin' (feminine form of 'Jüngling', 'youth'). By analogy with 'Fremdlingin' ('stranger') this rare archaic form occurs only in some earlier poets: i.e. Klopstock and Hölderlin.
p. 113	'Sleep' – probably dating from early summer of 1914 in Innsbruck.
p. 115	'The Thunderstorm' – written sometime between May and mid-July 1914. The poem bears a certain stylistic resemblance to the Storm and Stress odes of the young Goethe, though a contrast must be noted between the latter's expansive, life-affirming exuberance and Trakl's strenuously controlled diction, suggestive of a mind driven by, and wrestling with, its visions.
p. 117	'Evening' – written sometime during the early summer of 1914.
p. 117	'Night' – probably dating from the early part of July 1914. The incantatory opening and the poem's resonant hymnic style place it in the tradition of Klopstock and Hölderlin. *l.* 27 The concluding image, with its gesture of impetuous defiance towards the heavens, is evidently derivative of the myth of the Medusa.
p. 119	'Melancholy' – written in Innsbruck during June 1914. *l.* 22 'Mönchin' (female of 'Mönch', 'monk') is Trakl's own coinage: a word which conjures up a purer state of being, transcending the sexual, and one closely linked to the idea of death.
p. 121	'Homeward Journey' – written during June 1914. *l.* 8 'Anschaut' ('gazes') is arrestingly placed as the first word in the sentence. The resultant uncertainty as to subject and object lends added force to this key verb with its emphatic prefix (equivalent to *on–* in English).
p. 123	'Lament I' – written in Innsbruck and dating from July 1914. *l.* 6 'Traumbeschwerde' (literally 'dream-burden') is one of Trakl's neologisms.
p. 123	'Surrender to Night' – fifth version: written in Innsbruck during July 1914. In the previous (fourth) version of the poem the first line read: 'Nymphe zieh mich in dein Dunkel' ('Nymph draw me into your darkness'). *l.* 8 The phrase 'letzte Züge' ('final touches') has further connotations of dying, i.e. 'drawing one's last breath'.
p. 125	'In the East' – conceived during August 1914, probably in Innsbruck. *l.* 12 The verb 'brachen' ('broke, burst') is the first preterite within the poem, all previous verbs being in the present tense. The effect is that of the intrusion of an abrupt, unalterable event with its prospect of horror and violence.
p. 125	'Lament II' – written during September 1914. *l.* 4 'Verschlänge' constitutes a striking use of the subjunctive ('might or may devour') offering not a certainty but a possible outcome. *l.* 12 The dative is employed in an unusual construct involving the verb 'versinkt' ('is sinking') to establish a clear yet mysterious relationship between the subject 'boat' and the object 'Night'.
p. 127	'Grodek' – written in Cracow after 25 October 1914. The poem refers to the battle around Grodek in Galicia in early October 1914 where the Austrian army was in retreat and suffered heavy casualties. An earlier version, as reported by Ludwig von Ficker, did exist but is lost. *l.* 7 'Weidengrund' ('willow ground' or 'land on which willows grow') is not to be confused with 'Weidegrund' or 'Weideland' ('pastureland'). The willow is by tradition (and appropriately for this poem) a

tree signifying grief. *l.* 12 'Schwester' ('Sister'). It is often overlooked that Trakl pointedly uses the *impersonal* form in order to lend universal symbolic significance to this frequently introduced figure. 'Sister' may equally be applied to the religious or to nurses; countless 'Sisters of Mercy' commonly tended the wounded in the First World War. Nor is it plausible that this fastidious stylist should constantly resort to the familiar and colloquial form 'die Schwester' (meaning 'my sister') in all his poems. In a letter to Stefan Zweig (29 August 1915) Hugo von Hofmannsthal made the following comment about Trakl's last poem: 'Strange enough that he could make a poem out of his impressions of Grodek, in consequence of which, after all, he died.'

p. 127   'Revelation and Perdition' – This late prose poem was written in Innsbruck during May 1914. *l.* 4 'Fremdlingin' ('stranger': see note on 'The Heart' p. 111 above). *l.* 8, the adjective 'hären' (derivative of 'Haar', 'hair') meaning 'hairy' or 'of coarse hair' is recurrent in Trakl. Its suggestive meaning has connotations of harshness and self-chastisement as associated with the penitential 'hair shirt'. Cf. also line 2 of 'Rote Gesichter verschlang die Nacht', 'Afra' line 11, 'Ruh und Schweigen' line 3. *l.* 17 the word 'Leichnam' ('body, corpse') has a largely religious connotation here. It is, of course, customary to find a crucifix in the so-called 'Herrgottswinkel' ('God's corner') in every Austrian and Bavarian inn. *l.* 54 'das abgeschiedene Haupt' ('the secluded head') may also be rendered as 'the deceased head'.

p. 133   'St Peter's Churchyard' – published in the *Salzburger Volksblatt*, Year 39, no. 153, 10 July 1909. The poem is to be seen carved on a stone plaque at the eastern entrance to St Peter's Churchyard in Salzburg.

p. 133   'Night Soul' – third version: probably written after May 1914. First published in *Phöbus*, Year 1, no. 3, June 1914.

p. 137   'Song of Lament' – written in Salzburg and dated around late autumn 1911. Trakl wrote to Erhard von Buschbeck *à propos* of this poem: 'Enclosed the reworked poem. It is that much better than the original since it is now impersonal and full to bursting with movement and visions. I am convinced that it will speak and mean more to you in this universal form and manner than in the limited personal one of the first draft. You must believe me that it is no easy matter for me, and never will be, to submit unconditionally to what needs to be represented and I shall ever and again need to correct myself in order to give to truth what belongs to truth.'

p. 137   'A carpet wherein the suffering landscape pales' – dated between December 1912 and 17 February 1913. *l.* 2 'Gennesaret'; the reference is to the lake in the Holy Land where Simon Peter drew in the miraculous draught of fishes (Luke 5:1–5).

p. 139   'Delirium' – originally planned as part of a cycle entitled 'Delirien' of which only some fragments remain. Dated some time after 22 January and written in Innsbruck.

p. 139   'By the Rim of an Ancient Well' – second version: The earlier draft was entitled 'Am Rand eines alten Wassers' ('By the edge of an ancient pond') and was intended to form part of the 'Delirien' cycle.

p. 141	'The silence of the dead loves the ancient garden' – conceived probably not before 13 March 1913.
p. 141	'The blue night has risen gently upon our brows' – written between 23 May and August 1913.
p. 141	'O our dwelling in the silence of the twilit garden' – written between 23 May and 14 June 1913. *l.* 9 The phrase 'im Abend' ('within evening'), like line 2 'im Bruder' ('in her brother') expresses a deep state of indwelling which far transcends the bounds of conventional usage.
p. 143	'At Evening' – probably written in Vienna between 13 July and 16 August 1913.
p. 143–5	'To Novalis' – written either in 1913 or 1914, possibly not prior to September 1913. 'Novalis' is the pen-name of Friedrich von Hardenberg (1772–1801), an early Romantic poet and thinker. His *Hymns to Night*, the novel *Heinrich von Ofterdingen*, his religious lyrics and numerous aphorisms were seminal to the Romantic movement and later exerted considerable influence on European Symbolism. Through his novel Novalis introduced the mysterious 'blue flower' which was to become the central symbol of German Romanticism. The yearning for death, mystical union with the beloved beyond the grave, the higher reality of the dream, and the heightened consciousness induced by opiates, were among the congenial concepts which linked Trakl to Novalis.
p. 145	'Hour of Grief' – written between December 1913 and 6 March 1914.
p. 147	'To Lucifer' – certainly to be dated after 15 February and probably before April 1914. Lucifer, called 'the Light Bringer', is both the Morning Star and the Devil. Tradition has it that he, wisest and most beautiful of all angels, was cast out of Heaven for his pride and rebellion against God who thrust him down to the nether regions. It was the early Church Fathers who first identified Satan with Lucifer through their interpretation of Isaiah 14:12–19.
p. 147	'Red faces devoured by night' – probably written in June 1914.
p. 149	'Reverie' – written in Innsbruck, at the earliest in May and probably June 1914. *l.* 12 The subject of this sentence is left obscure: it might be read as an address to Night personified.
p. 151	'Psalm II' – written in Innsbruck at the earliest in May and possibly June 1914.
p. 151	'Autumn Homecoming' – third version: the first two versions were written in Innsbruck at the earliest in May 1914, shortly to be followed by the third. The first five lines are common to all three versions; a rare indication that the poet was satisfied with them.
p. 153	'Decline' – the first draft was probably written before 15 July 1914 in Innsbruck. It ended with the lines:

> Reich' deine Hand mir liebe Schwester
> In der Abendkühle.
> Give me your hand dear sister
> In the coolness of evening.

| p. 153 | 'Season of Life' – begun in Innsbruck in June or July 1914. |
| p. 153 | 'The Sunflowers' – written in Innsbruck in July 1914 at the latest. |

p. 155	'So grave o summer twilight' – written in Innsbruck during July 1914 at the latest. Some doubt exists within the manuscript as to the status of the word in the last line 'erblichene' ('faded') which might conceivably be read as 'erbliche' ('hereditary'), though this seems the less plausible reading.
p. 159	'Dreamland' – first published in *Salzburger Volksblatt*, Year 36, no. 109, 12 May 1906 pp. 2–4. The time of inception is not known.
p. 162	'Barabbas' – first published in *Salzburger Volksblatt*, Year 36, no. 147, 30 June 1906. The influence of Mallarmé's *Hérodiade* and of Oscar Wilde's *Salomé* has left its mark on the biblical tone and diction of this early lyrical prose.
p. 164	'Mary Magdalene. A Dialogue' – first published in *Salzburger Volksblatt*, Year 36, no. 159, 14 July 1906. The dominant contemporary influence of the Aesthetic Movement and of Decadence may be traced both in choice of subject-matter and in style.
p. 167	'Desolation' – first published in *Salzburger Zeitung*, no. 290, 20 December 1906. This early prose poem already points forward in its tone and treatment to characteristic features in Trakl's later development.

INDEX OF ENGLISH FIRST LINES AND TITLES

Titles are in bold, italic titles are first lines used as titles

INDEX OF GERMAN FIRST LINES AND TITLES